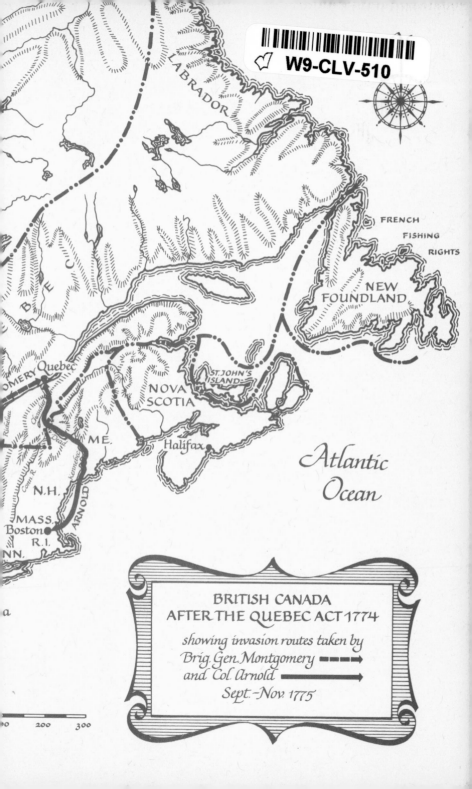

BRITISH CANADA
AFTER THE QUEBEC ACT 1774

showing invasion routes taken by
Brig.Gen.Montgomery ▪▪▪▪➤
and Col.Arnold ━━➤
Sept.-Nov. 1775

Attack on Quebec

Attack on Quebec

The American Invasion of Canada, 1775

Harrison Bird

New York • Oxford University Press • 1968

To the Memory of Nick Carroll (1885-1935)

a Woodsman who Taught Boys To Look and To See

Contents

The illustrations follow page 118

Maps

Attack on Quebec

I

Mission into Canada

Through a crack in the hen roost door Sergeant Bayze Wells could look out on a thin vertical slice of King George III's loyal province of Canada. He could see a corner of the farmhouse, thick-walled and foreign-looking, strange to a young soldier from Connecticut. The men had come out of the swamp the night before, 30 July 1775, tired, muddy, smelly, unshaven, insect-bitten, hungry, and thirsty. The major and the captain, who knew where they were going and what they were doing, had led the little troop of six men through a small square door into a low-ceilinged kitchen. The house was a safe one for Yankee spies, and the stubby brown Frenchman and his wife were friendly to *Bostonais* agents. The woman had poked up the fire and put the kettle of soup smelling of onions on to warm while her husband had fetched buckets of water so that his night visitors could wash and shave and refresh themselves after their journey.

Wells and the others had left the fort at Ticonderoga in a bateau eight days earlier. Sometimes sailing, mostly row-

ing, they had gone down Lake Champlain to its outlet into
the Richelieu River. There Sergeant Wells had hidden his
bateau, cached the extra stores (including the cask of rum),
and followed the officers into the Canadian bush. They had
come upon a horse, grazing in a riverbank meadow, and
on that warning of habitation the party had taken to the
swamp in which they floundered for three days and three
nights.

Now, through the crack in the door the sergeant could
see the chickens pecking gravel in the road. In the direction of the long morning shadows, the road led to the St.
Lawrence River and the ferry over it to Montreal. To the
east the road went to the towns of St. Jean and Chambly,
above and below the fast water that broke navigation between Lake Champlain and the St. Lawrence. The major
had sent his aide Peter Sherlon to the east to find the first
contact, a Mr. Minner, and bring him to the rendezvous.

In the dry chalky-white dust of the hen roost, Major
John Brown waited through the long July day. When Minner came, the major could start the work that he and his
team had come so far, and so stealthily, to do. Three months
before, thirteen British colonies on the Atlantic seaboard
had risen in armed rebellion against the oppressive measures
of the government of Great Britain. Only Canada and Nova
Scotia had remained aloof from the general uprising in
North America. Now the Continental Congress, the committee that co-ordinated the rebellion, was ready to move
against Canada with an army of liberation and an invitation to all right-minded Canadians to join the Congress as
the fourteenth colony. The major and his men were the ad-

vance agents of the army mustering at the far southern end of Lake Champlain.

Thirty-year-old John Brown was well qualified to lead the mission into Canada. He was a natural rebel. As an undergraduate at Yale College, Class of 1771, he had incited, organized, and led to a successful conclusion a student revolt against what he considered the appalling food served in the college "commons." On graduation, he had read law with the brother of his wife, Oliver Arnold, whose nephew (and therefore Brown's nephew by marriage) was the already noticeable young Benedict Arnold. After a brief tour as king's attorney in the Mohawk lands of the formidable old Tory, Sir William Johnson, Lawyer Brown had returned to his native Massachusetts. There, in the congenial Whigdom fulminating from the firebrands of Boston, John Brown's spark for rebellion kindled into flame. His first assignment from the Provincial Congress of Massachusetts, of which he was a member, was to lay a smoldering fuse of discontent in British Canada.

With the urgent press of time at his back, John Brown set out for Montreal with two companions in the face of a wintery February in 1775. Their way climbed the ladder of British defenses, each rung a fort: Ticonderoga, Crown Point, St. Jean, Chambly, connecting the Atlantic seaboard to Canada, the vast attic of North America. At the end of day, the lonely lights of the forts greeted the men, and the isolated soldiers of the garrisons gave welcome to the travelers, "buying Canadian horses for the American market." Methodically, John Brown counted the soldiers in each fort and noted the number of cannon that he saw.

Between the forts, the settlers of the Champlain Valley made room at their hearths for the member of the Massachusetts Congress and his companions. Neighbors came in to hear the news from Boston. On the east shore of Lake Champlain, Brown talked with the rough-hewn men of the Hampshire Grants. They called themselves Green Mountain Boys, and, like an ax handle to an axhead, they held true to their leader, John Brown's friend Ethan Allen. Where he traveled in New York State, Lawyer Brown moderated his voice. There the landholdings tended to large estates run as squirearchies in the lordly English manner.

Over the border in old French Canada, again the people were different. Here were peasants working the good grain land of the Richelieu River Valley, habitants set in their ways of language and religion and showing a convenient allegiance to their seigneurs because that was the amiable tradition. The fact that some of the seigneuries had been bought by English adventurers, up from the Atlantic seaboard, had little effect on the seasonal life of the *Canadien* farmer. Nor did it matter to the riverbank farmer that the corrupt economy of the French regime had been replaced in Montreal by greedy *Bostonais* merchants. It was to see one of these men that John Brown had made the long winter journey.

Thomas Walker, formerly of Boston, lived in his house at L'Assomption, outside the tumble-down walls of Montreal. Here Brown found him. In the prosperous comfort of the room into which the merchant led him, the two men talked far into the night. For the most part Walker listened, his bulk spilling over the arms of his chair. As

Brown told him of troopships coming into the Charles River and the stomp of military patrols in the night streets of Boston, Walker's fat fingers stroked the short gray hair above a torn and mangled ear. Ten years before in this very room a cloaked band of British officers, resentful of his merchant ways, had burst in, beaten him, and left him for dead among the wreckage of his furniture. Since that night, Thomas Walker flaunted the misshapen ear as a badge of contempt for all redcoats.

John Brown had little that was new to tell his host. In the normal course of commerce, Thomas Walker kept well informed. Every ship captain was a reporter of fact, every traveler a gossip. Only the summer before there had been a long visit from Benedict Arnold, who commanded a company of eager young patriots in Connecticut. In addition to talk, Walker had done good business with Arnold in a matter of horses, the West Indies, and smuggling. But the member of the Provincial Congress of Massachusetts was in Montreal not to buy, but to sell rebellion. He wanted Walker to organize and chair a Committee of Safety in Canada, and to link Canada to the other thirteen colonies by the couriers of a Committee of Correspondence; to all this the big merchant, his face in the guttering candlelight as red as the Cross of St. George, agreed.

John Brown had laid the train of powder from Boston to Montreal; Thomas Walker, in his house at L'Assomption, was to be the detonator. But as he journeyed back up Lake Champlain, Brown had doubted the will of the Canadians to rise in rebellion. This he reported to his colleagues of the Provincial Council.

Major Brown, a soldier since May, had been correct in his estimate of the temper of the Canadians. Walker's committee of merchants had not been strong enough to bring Canada into the armed conflict begun at Lexington and Concord. Hope of bringing the fourteenth colony into the rebel federation depended on invasion or, as it was deemed by the Continental Congress, liberation. Brown's second mission into British Canada was as a spy on a clandestine enemy mission, so throughout the long day he hid in the hen roost behind the safe house.

In the late afternoon Peter Sherlon brought Jan Minner to the rendezvous. The Albany Dutchman, whose role in the proposed invasion was to organize the commissary stores in the Richelieu Valley, had decided to go out with Brown's team and to report in person to the American general at Ticonderoga. Minner also alerted Brown to the danger of capture. Nevertheless, that night the team left the safe house on the Montreal road for another at Chambly.

The next day, 1 August, they went about their respective business. Peter Sherlon and Jan Minner set off for Montreal to see Walker. With them went a man whom Sergeant Wells knew only as Mr. Judd, to talk again with the chiefs at Caugnawaga. Brown and Captain Robert Cochran, an officer of the Green Mountain Boys and second in command to the major, made local contacts. They took with them the bundle of printed "Proclamations to the People of Canada" that the Continental Congress had phrased and that a subcommittee had translated into elegant French. Sergeant Bayze Wells, whose duties were those of security guard and water transportation, waited with the other two men in the safe house at Chambly.

The major and the captain returned separately before dark. Only ten minutes later a tap and a whisper at the door warned them that their cover was known and that the drums at the fort were beating assembly. From that moment the five Americans were on the run.

Loath to abandon Minner and Sherlon, John Brown ran a dodging, twisting, redoubling course that kept him close to Chambly. On 3 August the major sent one of his men, John Legger, to fetch the two from Montreal and to hide with them in a copse on the east bank of the Richelieu. The four remaining Americans sat down to rest and to wait in a cheerless camp. Seemingly from out of nowhere, a little French boy, smocked and holding a cattle goad, appeared and stood there, staring at the sprawled men. His mouth hung open, and fright was rising to replace the surprise in his wide eyes. Major Brown was the first to recognize the danger in the changing expression. He lunged, but the child was quicker, and ran screaming from the wood, Brown after him. Cochran, Wells, and the bateauman, last of the team, scrambled to their feet. Out in the field there was a great shouting and the men had a glimpse of the major standing tall in the midst of a menacing group of angry, gesticulating habitants. Brown was lost. Without hesitation, Captain Cochran ordered flight. No other way was open if even a part of the work of the wrecked mission was to be saved.

For four days the three survivors made their way east and

then south around the northern foot of Lake Champlain. On the fourth day they came to a creek which Cochran, who lived in the Hampshire Grants, swore he knew. Crossing it, they came to a logging road that would lead to Simon Metcalfe's mill and house. Still hunted, the three men cautiously approached the clearing where the house stood. They need not have been so wary. John Legger was splitting firewood at the block, Jan Minner sat sunning himself on the bench. Inside the house they found Peter Sherlon and the major, who had successfully talked and gesticulated his way out of his predicament with the local habitants.

Two hours before dark the reunited team left in a canoe, borrowed from Mr. Metcalfe, for Crown Point. They traveled at night, for the enemy were still out in search of them, and reached home without incident, seventeen days after they had started out.

In that time the army had grown. A semblance of order was emerging from the disorganized shambles the American camp had been. It only remained for John Brown to make his report to Major General Philip Schuyler; without delay, Brown hurried to headquarters at Ticonderoga.

Sergeant Bayze Wells was left to slip back into the old slothful ways of his regiment. But a new animation had taken over in the 4th Connecticut. Formerly idle men were working at their set tasks, guards were alert and well turned out, the junior officers marched about with an unwonted air of purpose. From the sergeant who offered Wells a blanket, a place in his tent, and a meal from the pot in exchange for an account of Canada, he learned that even affable, hail-fellow-well-met Colonel Benjamin Hinman had gone all soldier. During the time that Sergeant Wells had been away, General Schuyler had taken over command and had given the Northern Army a purpose in the proposed invasion of Canada.

2

Command on Lake Champlain

The sentry posted at the landing stage for Fort Ticonderoga took one look at Major General Philip Schuyler stepping out of the boat and fled into the guardroom. Presently the man returned to announce that he could not turn out the guard as required by protocol because he could not wake the men up. Schuyler was greeted with similar indolence at the next post, and at every stage of the way from the landing to the room where Colonel Hinman waited for someone to come to tell him to do something. Thus did the general of the Northern Army of the Continental Congress find the sharp edge of the command with which he was expected to invade Canada.

On 10 May, the day that Fort Ticonderoga had fallen into the hands of the rebels, Philip Schuyler had taken his seat among the other New York delegates to the 2nd Continental Congress at Philadelphia. He was a quiet delegate, respected in person and valued for his opinions on the affairs of his native Albany, the Indians of the lands to the west, and the great thoroughfare reaching northward to its junction with the St. Lawrence. The Congress had been in session for a week before word was received of the rape of the fort with its cannon and the governor's schooner. Major John Brown, lawyer and member of the Massachusetts Provincial Congress, made the report with his natural eloquence, backed by letter and emphasized by the display of the captured Union flag. The representatives of the rebellion in thirteen separate colonies listened in silence to the dramatic account of Ethan Allen's bold enterprise with his private army of Green Mountain Boys. They heard how the Committees of Safety in Connecticut and Massachusetts had combined with Allen of the Hampshire Grants to present Congress with the valuable gift of ordnance. Brown recounted his own mad dash into the fort as day was breaking, and mentioned the bravery of his colonel, James Easton, and the irresistible fury of the attack by the soldiery from the Green Mountains and from Massachusetts. Ethan Allen's official letter mentioned in passing that Colonel Benedict Arnold had entered the fort at his side.

When the ebullient Brown left the chamber, he left behind him the British flag. He also left the Congress in an embarrassing dilemma. The 2nd Continental Congress had forgathered with the hope that the armed rebellion could be confined to the affair at Lexington and Concord. In their discussions together, they had loyally separated the government of England from the person of their liege lord, the king. In the utterances of the Congress, the British soldiers penned inside Boston by the New England patriots were scrupulously referred to as the "ministerial troops." The guns seized at Lake Champlain, and the crossed flag of Union tossed so carelessly on the speaker's table were, however, the substance and symbol of the king's property. Ticonderoga had somehow turned a movement of justified rebellion toward one of revolution, where liberty wore the face of independence.

Ethan Allen's gift of two forts—Crown Point had fallen after Brown left for Philadelphia—also left in the reluctant hands of the Congress a weapon that menaced the Congress itself. The taking of the forts on the upper lake had reversed the direction of the sharp point of invasion along the Hudson-Lake Champlain thoroughfare. The pike shaft which formerly had had its butt firmly on the St. Lawrence was now turned around. Hands in New York State now held the power to lunge deep into the vitals of Canada.

In making the report of his winter journey to Montreal, John Brown told the Provincial Congress that the solid people of Canada were content with the king and parliament. Three months later the Continental Congress had no reason to believe that either by persuasion or by a thrust of arms would Canada join the rebellion. An invitation to take part in the 2nd Continental Congress had resulted in an observer being sent to Philadelphia by the minority merchant interests of Montreal. The acquisition of the strategical and tactically useful forts now prompted Congress to another invitation directed toward the French Canadians. A fine letter was drafted to the "Oppressed Inhabitants of Canada," asking them to join the thirteen Atlantic colonies "in defense of our common liberties, jeopardized by a licentious Ministry." In due course John Brown helped to deliver the

French translation of this cry for liberty. A more pressing
and positive document was then framed, passed by the Congress and sent north by fast courier. In their haste to disem-
barrass themselves of Ethen Allen's impetuous theft of the
king's cannon, the members ordered the guns to be se-
questered until harmony was restored between Britain and
the colonies.

Far away from the serious debates of Congress, on the remote shores of Lake Champlain the victors over Ticonderoga celebrated and fell out among themselves. Ethan
Allen, with his thundering voice and his private army of
Green Mountain Boys, had been the undoubted leader of
the attack. Colonel Easton and Major Brown, with their
few Massachusetts Minute Men and £300 of Connecticut
money, meekly accepted Allen's leadership. Not so Benedict Arnold, who arrived in a red uniform-coat, with a
valid commission as colonel from the Massachusetts Provincial Congress. All three factions had a claim to the insti-
gation of the expedition to capture the British forts, with
their precious ordnance. In reporting back to the Massachusetts Committee of Safety, Brown had urged the seizure of
the guns. On the basis of observations made while on his
trip to Montreal in 1774, Arnold had told the Connecticut
Committee that the cannon should be taken. And Ethan
Allen, who roamed the Hampshire Grants on the east shore
of Lake Champlain, knew the vulnerability of Fort Ticonderoga, just across the lake in New York, and conceived
its capture as another blow struck for Liberty.

Arnold's claim to leadership of the expedition against the

common objective was the weakest of the three. All he had was a respectable commission and valid orders. He had no troops, only £100, and the added disadvantage of arriving at the lakeshore only as the assault force was about to enter the boats. But in a heroic confrontation with the hulking Allen, the stocky colonel from Massachusetts (dressed in a Connecticut uniform) dominated the Green Mountaineer long enough to gain joint command of the venture. Allen even went so far as to present Arnold with a handy short blunderbuss with which to storm into the fort.

By mid-morning of 10 May, Benedict Arnold had lost all pretense of command. He had tried in vain to curb the riotous celebration and the wanton looting by the Green Mountain Boys, drunk with victory and the British captain's store of liquor. In his effort to impose military order in the captured fort, Arnold had failed to enlist the aid of Colonel Easton, a tavernkeeper, or of his "Uncle," Major Brown. By marrying into the Oliver Arnold family, Brown had assumed the contempt felt by the illustrious Providence Arnolds for the branch of the family in New Haven, and particularly for the scapegrace young Benedict. So on the day of victory Colonel Arnold sat alone with his thoughts— and his scheme. From the high prow of the north demilune of Fort Ticonderoga, Arnold could see the lake, brown and muddy here, as it flowed gently down toward Canada. As he sat in the sun, he wrote a letter to his friend Thomas Walker in Montreal. "I breakfast here," he wrote, "and expect soon to see you and your family in Montreal."

The means of delivering Arnold's letter arrived at Ticonderoga three days later: the schooner taken at Skenesborough, at the southern end of Lake Champlain. With her came some of Arnold's men, the first of an expected four hundred that Massachusetts had authorized the colonel to raise. Lying at anchor below the fort, the vessel suggested to Ethan Allen and the Connecticut faction a means of ridding themselves of the forceful Arnold, whose growing following threatened their position of command and control. For Benedict Arnold the schooner, swung around on her cable so that her bows pointed to the north, offered a chance to leave behind his failure to dominate at Ticonderoga and a vehicle in which to ride to a bold new enterprise. Somewhere down the lake was an armed sloop of the Royal Navy.

His feet once again on the planking of a quarterdeck (Arnold was a ship's master), a steersman beside him, taut sails drawing above him, a tow of bateaux trailing in his wake, "Commodore" Arnold sailed north. The British sloop was not to be found on the big lake. Without hesitation, and without any of the qualms and considerations that beset the Continental Congress, Benedict Arnold led his men across the vaguely defined border of New York onto the Richelieu River, where Canada began.

Rowing now in their bateaux, Arnold with thirty-five good men dropped downriver in the night. At dawn they saw the single tall mast of the sloop at her anchorage off the village of St. Jean. In minutes, one bateau was fast alongside the sloop, the other on shore, its crew running silently to surround the barracks which Arnold had pointed out to them. Within an hour the town was in rebel hands. Twenty-two British soldiers and sailors were prisoners. A squad of Americans was smashing British bateaux, while another squad loaded stores and readied the sloop for sailing. Colonel Arnold was in the town, listening to the few eager patriots, while silent groups of habitants stood about and watched them. Arnold learned that the naval lieutenant had gone to Chambly and on to Montreal for reinforcements. He was expected back that same morning with two hundred soldiers. Arnold did not wait. He had the sloop that he had come to fetch, and with it four big bateaux. He controlled all the boats of military use on all of Lake Champlain. Until the British could build another, stronger fleet, the forts and cannon at Ticonderoga and Crown Point were safe from counterattack. As Arnold, aboard the sloop—now renamed *Enterprise*—looked aft at the town of St. Jean slipping from sight behind a bend in the river, the gateway to Canada was ajar.

The first to enter was Ethan Allen. He had followed after Arnold with ninety of his Green Mountain Boys, loaded hastily and without provisions into four sturdy bateaux. They met the *Enterprise* six miles below St. Jean. While Allen and Arnold talked and drank in the sloop's cabin, the hungry men in the bateaux were fed. Though Arnold told him of the British reinforcements, he could not deter the big brash Green Mountain man from taking, and holding, St. Jean. For the second time that same day, 17 May 1755, the habitants of St. Jean saw their town occupied by the *Bostonais*. But Allen's thirst for compounding glory upon glory slackened as the two hundred British regulars drew near. He and his ninety men were gone from St. Jean before the file of drums passed the church and the mounted officer, in passing, doffed his hat to the priest standing in the open doorway.

On their return from St. Jean, Allen and Arnold kept apart, one at Ticonderoga and the other on board ship, cruising or at Crown Point. They were in accord, however, on one thing: that together they should seize, fortify, and hold a position at the nether end of the lake. Both were bent on invading Canada and taking Montreal, and perhaps Quebec City, too, as soon as Congress sent, to one or the other of them, troops and supplies.

Into the midst of these hopes and preparations the Continental Congress threw its stunning order to abandon the forts and remove the cannon into safekeeping. The incompatible twin heroes of the lake reacted by a frenzy of letter writing. Their importuning won support from New England and from New York, which in turn won a new order out of Philadelphia. On the last day of May the Continental Congress resolved that Connecticut be asked to supply the soldiers and New York the supplies necessary to hold the forts as a safe haven against attack by Britain and her Indians. This second order merely regularized a movement of Connecticut troops that already had begun.

Other men, jealous of the heroes, had been writing letters and reports and journeying to the seats of power. John Brown was in Philadelphia. James Easton had gone to Boston, where he had thoroughly undermined the Massachu-

setts Committee's confidence in their Colonel Arnold. By
mid-June, a committee was at the forts, investigating Arnold's conduct and scrutinizing his accounts. In indignation,
aggravated by a fever which was compounded when he
heard that his wife of nine years had died, Benedict Arnold
resigned his commission.

Of his enemies, only his old adversary Ethan Allen was
not watching from the windows of the fort as Arnold left
for home. The leader of the Green Mountain Boys had
gone to Philadelphia to regularize his men into a Congressional regiment of rangers with which he would conquer
Canada. The Connecticut faction, espoused by Easton and
Brown, was in command at the forts, over the fleet, and on
Lake Champlain as far as the Canadian border. Colonel
Benjamin Hinman had no one to dispute the authority
which he had no idea how to use.

The same Congress which in mid-May had been so
shocked by Ethan Allen's presumption in using its name to
steal the king's cannon, by mid-June had been forced into
a belligerent attitude. There was no curbing of the angry
New Englanders surrounding Boston, where the ministerial
troops lay licking their wounds after their disastrous march
toward Concord. New York was in trouble on her northern
border, where British Indians were a menace and where the
only other significant force of British troops was quartered.
Divided in sentiment between loyalists, patriots, and the
apathetic, and almost totally unprepared for armed rebellion, New York's cry for military help had been answered
by Connecticut, acting as an individual colony. With the

rise of fear and the spread of truculence, the Congress, which represented all thirteen aggrieved colonies, voted itself a Continental army.

On 15 June 1775 the Congress chose one of its members, George Washington, to be its general and commander in chief of all forces raised and to be raised. His first duty was to take charge of the siege of Boston and to make an army out of the rabble which he would find there. Four days later, at Washington's request, Philip Schuyler, also a delegate to the Congress, was commissioned major general for the especial trust of the independent command of an army in northern New York.

In all but physical appearance and the matter of health, George Washington and Philip Schuyler were the same cut of man. Each, in his early forties, was the product of almost a century of service to and industry in the colony to which his forebears had migrated. Both were born in wealth to command, and by experience both were natural in the habit of leadership. Each had served in the war of their youth, Washington with distinction on the frontier of his native Virginia, Schuyler as a regimental officer in New York. But whereas Washington was as a towering rock without fissure, Schuyler was a slim tree, deep-rooted and sturdy but buffeted by the harsh winds of chronic ill-health.

The two delegate-generals left the chamber of Congress together. Stirrup to stirrup, they rode across New Jersey. As they remounted at the landing place in New York City, Schuyler reined in behind his commander in chief for Washington's triumphal progress through the cheering

crowds that filled the streets. Four hours later, the same
fickle crowds turned out again to cheer the royal governor,
returned from a visit to London. From on top of his high
pedestal on the old bowling green, the statue of George III
looked down on both parades.

On parting, General Washington gave Major General
Schuyler his general orders. He was to watch well the activities of the royal governor; he was to concern himself with the friendliness or the neutrality of the Iroquois
Indians, whose lands lay west of Albany, he was to
make safe the defenses on Lake Champlain; and he was to
be ready to march against Canada if so directed. Before
Schuyler could reach his Albany headquarters, Congress
had implemented the final cautionary order into a direct
command to invade Canada. Ethan Allen had delivered his
harangue to the gentlemen in Congress.

At a desk covered with reports and letters, with an anteroom crowded with petitioners and visitors, Major General
Philip Schuyler set out to raise an army of men, with all the
supplies, munitions, and transport needed to take them to
Canada. Those who had gone before had given Schuyler the
invaluable gift of space and time. Allen, and Arnold too, by
their vision and prompt action had given the new major
general the forts halfway along the road from Albany to
Montreal. By taking the British sloop and bateaux at St.
Jean, Benedict Arnold had given Schuyler a further ninety
miles of the way to Canada. Arnold's American fleet had
bought time that the Americans needed to mount and
launch their invasion. Until the governor general could

build warships strong enough to defeat the fleet that Arnold had made on Lake Champlain, Schuyler had the time to build his army.

Somewhere between New York City and Albany, the two men passed each other. Schuyler was going north to assume his new responsibility. Arnold, ill, bereaved, and discredited, was going home.

3

Guy Carleton's Canada

Guy Carleton, governor of Quebec, was fifty years old when he returned to Canada in 1774 after four years of absence in England. The years he had been away, though quiet and orderly in his own province, had been years of ferment in British North America. In 1770, when Carleton left Quebec, a British army guard, badgered and frightened by a Boston mob, had perpetrated the "Boston Massacre." The year before the governor returned, another mob, this time dressed as Indians, had pitched three cargoes of taxed tea into Boston Harbor. In 1774, General Gage, commander in chief of the British forces in North America, concentrated virtually all of his troops, numbering more than ten thousand, in Boston. He was expecting trouble in enforcing the Boston Port Act, the coercive act of the patriot Whigs which closed the port in punishment for the Boston Tea Party. Thirteen of the fifteen British colonies in North America had called a congress in Philadelphia to unite in protest against the intolerable acts of the British ministers in Parliament. Although Guy Carleton's Province of Quebec had declined an invitation to participate in the 1st Continental Congress, it obviously was time for the governor to return to Canada.

Carleton's long visit at home had not been idle, neither in the public nor in his private interest. The dour old soldier-administrator with the grim mouth had found himself an aristocratic, vivacious young wife. Lady Maria Howard, the second daughter of the important Earl of Effingham, was thirty years her husband's junior. She was small and blonde, and her French, her manners, and her ability to flirt harmlessly had been learned at the French court, a fact which delighted her husband's subjects in Canada. The French seigneurs who made a miniature Versailles of the governor's court in Quebec heard and repeated a little history which made their governor's romance all the more charming. Rejected by the elder Howard sister, who later loved and married the governor's young nephew and aide-de-camp, the indomitable Carleton had won the true love of his little Maria.

Quebec City as viewed from the deck of the ship bringing Guy Carleton back from London was much as he had first seen it in 1759. Two tall headlands marked the place where the deep St. Lawrence estuary became a river flowing out of an immense land into the sea. Point Lévis guarded the south shore; Quebec City crowned the higher shore on the northern side. There was a tracing of fortress walls, the high sloping roofs of palaces, steeple-topped churches and chapels, and below the cliffs a smear of docks, warehouses, and mean dwellings at the waterfront. To the British soldiers crowding the decks of the transports that

summer of 1759, Quebec City had been an enemy citadel
to be stormed. It was as a conqueror that Lieutenant
Colonel Guy Carleton, quartermaster general of General
James Wolfe's victorious army, had entered the city. His
wounded head had throbbed under a swathe of bandages
the first time he had walked into the Château de Louis
which, fifteen years later, was his gubernatorial palace and
his home.

Carleton's homecoming in 1774 was as triumphal as had
been his entry into Quebec City after the battle on the
Plains of Abraham in 1759. He was made welcome by the
French people, the former enemy, who still lived there and
who respected their English governor and general for his
fair and sympathetic rule. For the French subjects of the
British crown in Canada, Governor Carleton brought from
London, like a bright new banner, the Articles of the Quebec Act.

During the four years that Governor Carleton had been
away he had been lobbying for "An Act for making more
Effectual Provision for the Government of the Province of
Quebec, in North America." The "Quebec Act," which
embodied the respect held by the British military for the
French Canadians and their institutions, received the king's
assent on 22 June 1774. The act's rapid passage through
Commons and Lords was speeded by the determination of
Parliament to keep loyal to the crown one ethnic group and
one colony in turbulent North America.

The thirteen restive colonies which had united in a rebel-
lious congress immediately marked the Quebec Act as yet

another "intolerable act." By one of its articles the southwestern border of Quebec Province was placed in the Ohio Valley. This was the very land that Virginians and Pennsylvanians had won from French Canada in the old war. The Ohio Valley was Indian land, coveted by pioneers for a new colony already curiously named "Vandalia," in honor of Queen Charlotte's Vandal ancestors. The Quebec Act handed the land back to the Indians, who even that summer were on the warpath. Chief Logan, a Mingo, had been goaded to terrible vengeance by the murder of his mother and eight other Indians while they lay drunk in a frontier tavern. It was the temper of the seaboard colonies that their anger flew off in all directions. Only the most bitter Indian-hating frontiersman could condone the murders. The governor of Virginia was held a brute, a ministerial brute, for sending troops against the Mingos, who took their own bloody revenge. The same heads and tongues that gave Governor Dunmore's name to the unpopular war rationalized that it was the Quebec Act that had sent Logan burning and scalping on the Ohio.

To the righteous New Englander whose scalp lock was his religious conscience, the popish cross was more of a menace than was the Indian's tomahawk. By guaranteeing the French Canadians liberty to profess their Roman Catholicism, the Quebec Act raised the hackles of the New England watchdog of Puritanism, who howled his angry protest.

Even more shocking than its betrayal of Protestantism was the Act's granting to Canada the usage of French law in civil cases. This suspension of trial by jury was a blow at every Englishman's most cherished right and tradition. The disaffected in the thirteen seaboard colonies made the most of these instances of ministerial irresponsibility and exported their arguments to the prospective fourteenth colony as propaganda.

A fourth article of the Quebec Act hit home to the Anglo-Canadian merchants, concentrated in the commercial city of Montreal. The government of Canada was to be by governor and council, without an elected assembly. The merchants were indignant. They had rushed up from the Atlantic colonies to fill the vacuum left by the economic collapse that had followed the fall of New France. The merchants expected electoral preferment as well as fortune, but they were only a minuscule minority, despised as mere tradesmen by the British military who governed Canada through an impartial council.

Governor Guy Carleton took little notice of the intrigues of the merchants. Thomas Walker, their leader, openly received his visitors from the south, yet he was allowed to walk the streets of Montreal at liberty. Carleton administered his Quebec Act and governed Canada from Quebec city through his military colleagues, the former French seigneurs, and Bishop Briand of Quebec.

The affair which occurred in Montreal on 1 May 1755 scarcely troubled the calm rule of Carleton's Canada. There had been time for news of a skirmish at Lexington to be brought north. Working people who crossed the Parade in the early morning were the first to see how the bust of

George III had been decorated. During the night the statue, which stood in a little pergola, had been painted mourning black. A bishop's mitre had been placed slightly askew on the king's head, and around his neck was a rosary of old potatoes from which dangled a wooden cross. A label completed the desecration: Voilà le pape du Canada, le sot Anglais (This is the pope of Canada and the fool of England).

Within minutes the Grenadier Company of the 26th Foot had been called out. They came at the double, their equipment jangling, to form up around the pergola and keep the crowds back. Soon drums were beating through the town, announcing a reward of two hundred dollars to anyone discovering the offender. British officers, gathered on the Parade, pointed to the "fanatick" merchants. Thomas Walker promptly disavowed the vandalism on behalf of his friends by proclaiming a second reward.

The tension of the day mounted with the sun. Roman Catholics took religious offense and accused the Jewish community. In one corner of the square a Jew struck a habitant. Both were hurried away. Elsewhere a "Canadien" pulled the nose of an Englishman and was knocked down for his effrontery. François Marie de Belestre, the French Canadian militia leader, scuffled with a young visitor from Philadelphia, who was promptly arrested and thrown into jail where he was kept without bail. The mob, growing now, and excited, made a martyr of the young *Bostonais* whose rights of habeas corpus had been denied. A judge was hastily summoned, and he immediately released the prisoner. The excitement was over. The marble bust of George III was cleaned as well as possible. No one claimed the rewards.

Governor Carleton did not consider the incident in Montreal of enough significance for him to leave Quebec City. Neither the desecration of the statue nor the factional brawls attending it were indications of a crack in the internal security of Canada. The Quebec Act and the years of co-operative occupation by the British military had given a patina of calm to the ninety thousand habitants subject to the crown. The strident merchants were few enough to be ignored.

By every logical argument Canada seemed free of any thought of invasion. The militant patriots taunting General Gage in Boston, and the speech-making politicians meeting in Philadelphia were remote. Dunmore's War on the distant Ohio was the concern of the governor of Virginia and of Carleton's reliable Indian agents. The sea approaches to Quebec City, the traditional direction of attack, were well guarded by the British navy out of its base at Halifax in Nova Scotia. Montreal, at the head of Lake Champlain, could be attacked from the south, but there was no army in that direction. The officer stationed at Ticonderoga reported the neighborhood quiet and orderly.

Though Ticonderoga, Crown Point, and Lake Champlain were in New York, practical considerations placed them within the military sphere of the governor of Quebec, who also was general in chief of all Canada. In reviewing the defenses of Canada, he recommended that the forts at Ticonderoga, Crown Point, and also on Lake George be repaired. He suggested, too, plans for improving the "flimsy" walls of Montreal and restoring the defenses of Quebec to their former strength. In his report to London, Carleton estimated that to defend Canada against an invading army would require ten thousand men, with engineers and artillerists in addition. But as there was no enemy to be seen, nothing had yet been done by 1775. In fact, General Gage, the commander in chief of all the British forces in North America, had drawn on Carleton for troops to be sent to Boston. On 4 September 1774, Carleton sent away the two best regiments of the four that he had under command.

For the defense requirements of Canada, Governor Carleton relied on the Canadian militia to support the scant one thousand British regulars left to him. His staff estimates showed a potential eighteen thousand stout habitants, many of whom had had military training under the French. Carleton and the other British officers who had fought against the Canadiens in the old war idealized them as soldiers. The continental French, however, had referred to the militia as *chouayens*, meaning "skulkers."

They were still *chouayens*, in 1775, when their British masters called on them to organize, as the now-departed French had done. The Quebec Act had not reached down its helping hand to the habitant farmer of the St. Lawrence Valley, who would constitute the majority of Carleton's eighteen thousand eager militiamen. The habitant still had to pay his tithe to the Church; he still had to work out his taxes on the call up to labor. In general, he hated the rich, landowning seigneurs, the relics of French feudalism whom Carleton designated as the officers of the rural militia. In Terrebonne, north of Montreal, the habitants drove their seigneur away with scythes and pitchforks when he tried to muster them.

Carleton turned to the Church. Bishop Briand issued a *mandement* telling the people to support the "good, gentle king of England." The parish priests who read the *mandement* to their people explained it in different terms. They preferred to shelter their habitant congregations from the exposure by service to Protestants; then, too, they wished to keep alive the fear of those other Protestants, the *Bostonais*.

The governor, acting in his capacity as general, was busy with defenses when the spring thaw came to Lake Champlain and the ice went drifting down the St. Lawrence to the sea. He had two understrength regiments with many old men in their ranks. The 26th was at Montreal, with garrisons up Lake Champlain. The 7th was with him in Quebec City, where his influence had raised two militia regiments, one French-speaking, the other taking orders given in the English tongue. M. Belestre, who had scuffled with the young Philadelphian, had organized a militia company of eighty men in Montreal. They were soon to turn out to drive Ethan Allen and his boys from St. Jean.

Guy Carleton was fortunate in having in Montreal that spring a very redoubtable Scotsman named Allan Maclean. A veteran of 1759, Maclean had been given permission to raise two battalions of highlanders from among the Scots who were settled in North America. With pipes, a dram of whisky, and a jocular brogue, old Maclean had recruited four hundred likely Scots in New York State. His major was beating the ribboned drum for the 2nd battalion in Nova Scotia. Lieuteant Colonel Maclean lost most of his New York Highlanders when the rebels closed the road to the gathering place in Canada. In Montreal, however, he found three hundred and fifty men and the retired officers that he needed for the Royal Highland Emigrants.

On Friday morning, 19 May 1775, Guy Carleton was early at his desk in his palace high on the rock that is the formidable City of Quebec. Any hopes that the younger members of his staff might have had for a long weekend with their salmon rods were shattered by the arrival of the dispatch boat from Boston. The orders that the courier brought were as explicit as they were alarming: all the regular forces in Canada were to take up a strong defensive position on the Richelieu River, facing south. The rebellion was expected to spread.

All that day the governor, wearing his general's uniform, was busy. The 7th Foot (the Fusileers) had to be uprooted from their good billets in the city and sent west. Arrangements must be made and transport provided for the 7th to pick up the garrison at Trois Rivières. Orders had to be written and sent to Montreal so that the 26th Foot would go at once to St. Jean. Captain Hector Theophilus Cramahé, the lieutenant governor of Quebec City, had to be briefed in the government and defenses of the city during Carleton's absence. The governor and general was moving himself, and therefore the government of all Canada, to Montreal.

The pressure continued on into the next day. Into the hurried goings and comings in the governor's ante-room came the second important messenger in as many days. Moses Hazen, born in Massachusetts of Jewish parents, was a retired British officer with claims on Carleton's friendship dating from the Louisbourg and Quebec campaigns of 1758 and 1759. Hazen had bought a modest seigneury on the Richelieu River, when its owner had chosen to return to France. Traveling hard and fast, Moses Hazen had come the one hundred and thirty-odd miles from his manor house to the Château de Louis in two and one-half days. He was eager to be the first to tell his old comrade the terrible news from Lake Champlain: how Ticonderoga and Crown Point had been lost to the rebels; how one Benedict Arnold had captured and taken away the king's sloop; how only the timely arrival of troops from Montreal had saved St. Jean from the bellowing Ethan Allen. Moses Hazen with his tale of disaster beat the official courier to Quebec City by a day. On 23 May, Governor Carleton left the capital city of Canada. The effectives of the 7th Foot went with him.

The regiment left behind only their sick and the aged men. With the few gunners, who tended the stores and kept the songbirds from nesting in the rows of cannon on the city walls, there remained only sixty-one soldiers of the regular establishment in the fortress of Quebec. Twenty-six additional fusileers were on outpost duty; there had not been time to send and fetch them, and besides, they were needed where they were, up the Chaudière River.

Across from and about nine miles above Quebec City, the Chaudière enters the St. Lawrence in the "boiling" rapids and the falls that give the river its name. It is a quiet river as it crosses the St. Lawrence plain. From the last settlement to its source in Chaudière pond—Lake Megantic, as the Indians called it—the river boils again for some eighty-seven miles. South of the tangle of swamps and streams that gather to make Lake Megantic, low mountains trace their peaks and ridges in a jagged line across the sky. It was told that the Abenaki Indians, from the province of Maine in Massachusetts Colony, came down from the Height of Land to hunt and to visit with the northern Abenaki of the St. Lawrence.

In 1760, the engineer, Lieutenant John Montresor, in an incredible journey, proved the Indian tale to be true. With thirteen rangers, Montresor ascended the Chaudière, crossed over the Height of Land, and after days of wandering and near starvation in a frozen maze of ponds and streams, morass and forest tangle, found the Kennebec River, which took him down to the coast of Maine. One man had frozen to death. The following summer Lieutenant Montresor had made the journey again, to map the waterways on the New England side of the Height of Land. That, too, had been an arduous journey through a cruel land. However, the way through the mountains was a road, an almost secret road, between the Atlantic and the St. Lawrence, and the governor in Quebec had set a watch over it. He wished to know of the comings and goings of the Abenaki, and to learn the business of any New England woodsmen who might dare the long way that Montresor had mapped.

The twenty-six soldiers of the 7th Foot were in the upper settlements of the Chaudière when the regiment went west. They would summer where they were, returning to Quebec City when the autumn storms closed the Indian trail to Maine.

4

Overland to Quebec City

Lieutenant John Montresor was penned up in Boston with Gage's army while his map of the overland way to Quebec was receiving flattering attention at the headquarters of the rebel General Washington in Cambridge, over the Charles River. When spread out over a staff table, the copy of the British engineer officer's finely drawn map showed the Kennebec River in all its convolutions. The place of the great carry across to the tributary Dead River, well described in Montresor's accompanying journal, was clearly marked. The massive mountain with the long Indian name was there as a reference point for the northward bound traveler seeking the west branch of the Dead River. The Height of Land was a nicely shaded row of small peaked mountains, looking little higher than a fold-crease in the tablecloth when the general sat down to dine. Above the line of hills lay Lake Megantic, with a tadpole's tail of the Chaudière wriggling across the plain to Quebec City where every eye lingered.

The attack on Quebec City, the hive of Indian raids, the tabernacle of popery, was never far from the thoughts of the New Englanders. At the outset of every colonial war, plans were made for an attack on Quebec. The feint at Boston anticipated an attack from there. The right way to assault Quebec was Wolfe's way: by a sea-borne invasion. With the help of the British Navy, Massachusetts Colony twice had tried the sea route, and twice, through misadventure, had failed. The overland route by the Kennebec-Chaudière or, inversely, by the Chaudière-Kennebec, was always a hope or a dread. As early as 1697, Iberville, the boldest of Canadians, had planned with Castine to attack Boston through Maine, where the latter claimed a seigneury. Since that time forts and soldiers had guarded the Kennebec River. In 1775, anxious Maine men sent watchers upriver, just as Carleton kept his outpost on the Chaudière. In 1756, the British commander in chief, who was also governor of Massachusetts, prepared a plan for two thousand soldiers to march to Quebec over the Height of Land. Before Washington took command on 2 July 1775, a less ambitious but more confident plan of attack had been discussed in the rebel camp at Cambridge in Massachusetts. Colonel Jonathan Brewer, who had been an officer in the Ranging Service and spoke knowingly of the overland trail, vowed that, given five hundred volunteers, he could go to Quebec and take the city "with felicity."

The Montresor map in General Washington's headquarters gave credence to the old ranger's boast. The Indians, too, who came in their smelly blankets to see and assay the rebel general, confirmed all prior knowledge of the route. The chiefs from St. Francis on the St. Lawrence side of the mountains (the ones who had counted only eight British regulars in all Quebec City) minimized the hardships of their own journey to Cambridge. The Penobscot Indians, who were in Cambridge as volunteers, could tell of crossing the Height of Land by the Kennebec route with their women and children and dogs for an annual hunt. But Washington scarcely listened to these friendly Indians, whose leader was a renegade white man. He missed the usual caution in their account of the route, and ignored their proffered help as guides and hunters of food.

Washington had come to believe in the need for an overland attack on Quebec. Such an attack would be a diversion for General Schuyler's expedition against Montreal. As the plan matured, in discussions over Montresor's map and when the staff officers gathered in the long evenings of July, the diversion grew into a second invasion, with the capture of Quebec City an accepted conclusion. As July became August, less and less was heard about Washington's other scheme: an invasion of Nova Scotia. All attention at headquarters centered now upon the Quebec plan.

Before giving his final assent, General Washington wished to have the approval of General Schuyler, to whom the invasion of Canada already had been entrusted. On 20 August, Washington wrote in enthusiastic terms to his friend and subordinate on the northern frontier. While he was waiting for a reply, preparations for the Kennebec were put in hand.

The job of finding the one thousand to twelve hundred men allotted for the venture fell to the adjutant general, Horatio Gates. In assembling his staff, George Washington

was fortunate in finding such a thorough professional soldier for the appointment of adjutant general. Gates had
been living in Virginia in disgruntled retirement, his abilities
as a staff officer having outrun his social position and therefore his chances of promotion in the British Army. A commission of brigadier general revitalized the elderly-looking
veteran of '45, who immediately threw himself into the
work of creating a Continental army.

Gates was a shrewd judge of men, and he recognized the
potential in Benedict Arnold, who, in the summer of 1775,
found his way to the adjutant general's office. Arnold had
a scheme for attacking Quebec overland by way of the
Kennebec and Chaudière rivers. Gates, who was also a
politician, espoused his protégé and his plan, and at just
the right moment, presented Benedict Arnold to the attention of Washington.

* * *

For the four months since Lexington and Concord, Benedict Arnold had fought to fight. His opponents had been
the cautious, the jealous, the envious, the skeptical. The
fact that, on Lake Champlain, he had encountered his uncle-
by-marriage, John Brown, was unfortunate for Arnold.
Though the two men were of an age, the nephew was not
as well versed as the uncle in the political niceties required
to achieve personal ends by patient means. As a direct
descendant of the first Arnold in the New World, Benedict
could walk erect without a rival and show his scorn of
jealously by his confident step. However, he was as vul-

nerable to scandal as he was contemptuous of the stumbling blocks put in his way by an intense family rivalry.

The Arnold family was old in the new world of North America, where it was distinguished by wealth and high position in the colony of Rhode Island. Benedict was the fourth of his name and the fifth of his line in North America. It was his father who had removed to Connecticut, leaving his brother Oliver to continue in the family's native colony. The Arnolds at home grew disapproving as the Connecticut branch prospered in the new environment. Everything the young Benedict did took on ominous proportions as family news trickled back to Newport, Rhode Island. The dark-complexioned scapegrace son of Benedict III (who was rumored to be "drinking") had twice run away to join the army on Lake Champlain, and had twice come home again without his captain's leave. He was reported to his Uncle Oliver to be a brawler and a dueler as well as a coxcomb. The Rhode Island Arnolds, who upheld the law, looked askance, too, at Benedict's activities as a smuggler, something which in others was considered to be a patriotic duty that contravened the intolerable Stamp Act. That young Benedict, head of the family since his father's death, was once near bankruptcy was longer remembered in Rhode Island than the fact that he worked his own way out of his financial troubles.

Alone and unencumbered by wide family obligations and dignities Benedict Arnold had made a good life for himself in New Haven. The ships that he had inherited, and which he sometimes sailed himself, had increased and prospered. They carried his trade goods, mostly fat horses, from Can-

ada to the West Indies, and brought back to the northeast
coast produce and various imports. In all these places
Arnold became a familiar figure and a welcome guest. At
home in New Haven he had friends and commanded respect. His marriage in 1767 to the daughter of the county
sheriff was an event of that year. Margaret bore him three
sons, and kept his house in New Haven while he traveled
on sea or land, and it was from this home that she saw her
husband off to war.

It happened all of an April afternoon. The Committee
of Safety's rider, who came from Worcester in a day and
a half and two nights, arrived on the college green in the
early afternoon of 21 April. His message, first read from
the saddle, was simple news: the British soldiers, a thousand
strong, had come out of Boston and had marched to Lexington, where a company of militia was drawn up on the green.
Without provocation, the regulars had fired into the militia,
killing six men and wounding four.

There was no cry for help in this first telling of the news
from Massachusetts. Benedict Arnold, who had hurried to
the green, needed no such call. About a month earlier, he
had been complimented with the commission of captain in
the 2nd Company of Governor's Foot Guards. Now, while
the crowd milled about and the courier slaked his thirst,
Captain Arnold beat the assembly drum for his company.
They came running, the smart young men of the town
and the eager students from Yale College. As the townspeople hushed, Arnold addressed his soldiers. They were
to go home, get into their uniforms, don their accouter-
ments, and reassemble in an hour with their blankets to

march toward Boston. With a cheer, the young men broke ranks to obey.

Within the hour they were back, a smart military line of three ranks of red-coated soldiers stretched across the green. Quiet women and girls stood beside their men while younger brothers ran about or stood, looking enviously at the soldiers. A few of the students without uniform gathered on the left of the line. Behind them the wagons were drawing up, with the "Way there!" and the "Haw!" of the drivers loud above the babble of voices.

The first stop for the company was the town magazine, there to fill the men's pouches with paper cartridges and to load the wagons with kegs of powder and bars of lead. Here, before the iron-bound door, Benedict Arnold was first confronted by hesitant authority. Up to this point, Arnold had followed his own true instinct to action. At the powder house he was forbidden entry: General David Wooster refused Captain Arnold the key. As general commanding all the Connecticut militia, the sixty-four-year-old veteran of two colonial wars (of which he reminisced incessantly) claimed that he lacked the authority to release the stores. Feebly, old General Wooster temporized for caution and delay. There had been no holding back by the Lexington militia when they formed up on their village green. Six dead, all militiamen like themselves, were authority enough for the 2nd Company of Governor's Foot Guards; Arnold got his powder from the colony's stores.

Benedict Arnold found no action imminent around Boston. The British, after their sortie to Lexington and Concord, appeared content to stay in the city. In the rebel camp at Cambridge, where the Governor's Foot Guards had pitched their tents, all was confusion and ardor without direction. From all over New England musketmen came daily, in companies, in bands, or singly, to swell the mass of indignant citizens. In this ruck a simple captain of a single company of Connecticut militia could sink without a trace.

Arnold's alternative to oblivion lay in his own restless self and in his leading ambition. He was like one of his stallions, newly bought in Canada, who, having run free into the dockside loading pen, finds himself enclosed. He paused only long enough to set a new goal, gather his energies, then rush the fence. To become an army, to drive the British soldiers out of Boston, to achieve liberty, the crowd of musketmen sprouting like spring grass on the Cambridge hills needed cannon. Arnold knew where the cannon were; he had seen them lying, virtually untended, at the Lake Champlain forts. To go there, to get the guns, to bring them to Cambridge, Benedict Arnold needed authority to recruit an army and credit to pay its expenses. He found both in the Massachusetts Committee of Safety, which was conducting the siege of Boston. Within a fortnight, Arnold was off at a gallop to the northern lakes and his bold enterprise in that direction. He was no longer the captain of a fashionable company of Connecticut militia. He was a colonel, commissioned by and under orders from Massachusetts.

Three months later Benedict Arnold was back in Cambridge, his fortune and his fame having run full cycle. On his expedition north he had fought for liberty, won himself a navy, and pushed ajar the gate to Canada. But before he could gather his forces to fling wide the gate and enter, he was tied and hobbled, and finally, broken in health and spirit, returned to New Haven.

Even in a home that was saddened and emptied by the death of his wife, Arnold's resilience asserted itself in renewed determination. In Margaret's place in his home, charged with the management of his children and his affairs (including a vessel at sea, bound for Quebec City), he installed his sister Hannah. Dragged back from Montreal, he was now free to pursue his new objective: Quebec City. First, however, he had to justify himself before the Massachusetts Committee of Safety, which had trusted him and then withdrawn that trust while he was on Lake Champlain.

Though the sprawling, brawling, untidy camp at Cambridge was much the same as when he had last seen it, there was a new spirit in the place. George Washington had come to Cambridge with his general's commission, his little staff of officers, and his presence. In Washington there was leadership to raise hope, discipline to achieve direction, and purpose to attain the goal. Benedict Arnold, while he was settling his accounts with the committee, found congenial company with kindred ambitions around the commander in chief's headquarters. Horatio Gates took into his circle the sometime captain, former colonel.

At the moment when George Washington was ready to choose a leader for the invasion of Canada by way of the Height of Land, Gates presented Benedict Arnold. Though he was scarcely a soldier by professional standards, Arnold was a proven leader whom men followed. He also knew

Canada and Canadians, from Montreal to the fortress of
Quebec City, and he had friends on the lower Kennebec
River, where his own schooner had anchored to trade. On
his introduction to Washington, he immediately presented
his plan, based on a copy of Montresor's map, for an attack
on Quebec City by the overland route.

On 1 September 1775, General Washington appointed
Benedict Arnold a colonel in the Continental Army. Five
days later, the intent to send an expedition overland to
Quebec was published in General Orders. This was ten
days after Arnold, still ostensibly a civilian, from a writing
table at headquarters had started work on his expedition
up the Kennebec.

There were innumerable questions for which the designated commander had to find the answers: How soon, and
at what cost, could two hundred light bateaux be built,
each with four oars, two paddles and two setting poles?
What quantities of meat, both fresh and salt, and what flour
could be assembled on the Kennebec? Had the summer
weather on the upper Kennebec been dry, or wet enough
to float the bateaux? Could a party go at once to the upper
Kennebec to blaze the old carrying trails? Arnold addressed
these and countless other questions to his acquaintance,
Reuben Colburn, boatbuilder and factor of Gardinerstown,
on the Kennebec. While he waited for the answers, Arnold
sat along with Horatio Gates, compiling tables of organization and finding "bodies" for the army of expedition. Alone
at night Benedict Arnold again and again went over the
timetable of his advance on Quebec.

Much was accomplished between 21 August, when Arnold took over the plan, and the day that the expedition was announced in General Orders. General Washington had, in effect, approved of the attack on Quebec on the day that he wrote to Philip Schuyler. Until the commander of the Northern Army gave his approval to plans for a second and concurrent front in Canada, Washington, ever the courteous gentleman and considerate officer, withheld his final assent.

5

General Schuyler's Army

When Philip Schuyler went north to invade Canada he was a general without an army, a commander without troops. His only asset was one retired British Army captain who, in accepting a brigadier general's commission, had stepped from loyalty to treason. Like Washington, Schuyler understood his own limits as a general officer, and like the commander in chief who had found the former British staff officer Horatio Gates to help him, the commander in the north found Richard Montgomery ready to join in the rebellion for political liberty.

The son of an Irish baronet, Montgomery was tall and, in spite of a pock-marked face, he was well-favored and handsome. After a military career which began in 1754 at the age of eighteen and ended voluntarily after the conquest of French Canada, Montgomery returned to England, where the young Irishman's liberal ideas brought him close to the great Whigs in Parliament. In 1772, he uprooted himself and emigrated to New York Colony, where he bought a small estate in the mid-Hudson Valley. A year later, he married the daughter of Robert Livingston, who, as a lord of the manor, was as aristocratic in Scottish descent as were the Schuylers in descent from the Dutch. Richard Montgomery brought to the Whig rebellion in New York a valuable contact with the Parliamentary Opposition in London. To Major General Philip Schuyler, he brought experience gained as adjutant of his old regiment, as well as knowledge acquired in the 1760 invasion of Canada over the route from Ticonderoga to St. Jean to Montreal. Brigadier General Montgomery early gave evidence of his courage, both physical and moral, a quality so greatly needed in New York Colony in 1775. His very leavetaking from home was the occasion for entreaties and tears enough to rust the keenest cavalry saber. The protests of his devoted wife followed Montgomery north to Ticonderoga, where the instances of delay and frustration were enough to make a less resolute soldier cry out in despair.

The extent to which New York was unprepared for the war that was thrust upon it was quickly made clear to Schuyler and Montgomery. The four regiments authorized in June by the New York Committee of Safety were not forthcoming in July, despite General Schuyler's entreaties. The Committee's excuse was a valid one: it did not have the money to equip, to maintain, or to send north the men they had as soldiers entitled to the name. It was to be another month, the latter part of August, the end of summer, before the first four companies of the New York contingent were to arrive at Ticonderoga.

The New Yorkers were made welcome to the lakes by the sneers of the incumbent veterans from Connecticut. A

pattern of intercolonial jealousy soon developed. Since the
two Continental generals had arrived in mid-July, Colonel
Hinman's demoralized regiment had regained its pride, and
under Montgomery's professional guidance, even the colonel had shown some competence as an officer. Much work
had been done in the newly inspired fever of haste. Enough
bateaux had been built to carry the first wave of the invasion
across Lake Champlain. Stores for twenty days had been
stockpiled. A sixty-foot boat had been nearly completed
by the end of July, and another had been laid down. The
vessels of Benedict Arnold's fleet, their crews newly ani-
mated, were on constant station down the lake. The spies
and agents that Schuyler sent north checked in and out on
board the *Liberty* and the *Enterprise*. By careful gleaning,
there was plenty of news to be had out of Canada. In the
Richelieu River Valley, where Schuyler expected to fight
the decisive battle for Montreal, there were situations
which, if properly developed, could materially assist the
invading army. A Livingston cousin of Montgomery's wife
lived there, and Moses Hazen, who had carried the news
to Governor Carleton, was now ready to favor the rebel
cause. On the seigneuries of both, as well as on smaller
holdings, a crop to sustain an army of "liberation" was
maturing. Agents were negotiating the future harvest with
coins of patriotism and papers promising cash. Montgomery's spies were bringing in a treasure of military intelligence from St. Jean. The American generals knew of the
new fort being built there, and knew that it incorporated
within its earth and stockade walls two strong points. Of
most concern to the Americans at the southern end of Lake

Champlain was the progress made in the building of two British warships at St. Jean. From across the Richelieu River one had a good view of the ribs rising out of the keel, and as the planks enclosed the hull, the burden of the new vessels became evident. The shape, size, and length of the mast and spars lying in the grass at the back of the yard told how the craft were to be rigged. There were numerous indications—gun ports, ships' carriages, pieces—to tell the alert spy the number of guns each warship would carry. All these reports and estimates, when sifted at Ticonderoga, added up to two vessels that, when launched, could take back from Benedict Arnold's fleet the naval dominance of Lake Champlain. Two such warships as were building at St. Jean, once free on the lake, could annihilate the American invasion flotilla.

Schuyler and Montgomery knew, too, the disposition that Guy Carleton had made of his regular troops: four hundred and seventy British soldiers at St. Jean, plus M. Belestre's company of Canadian militia; one hundred and ten regulars at the old stone fort at Chambly, ten miles further down the river. The turning out of the other Canadians in militia companies was the concern of both British and American commanders. By law and by inducements and by the bishop's intercession, Governor Carleton had failed to muster more than a modicum of the eighteen thousand musketeers that he had once estimated as being available to him. General Schuyler's propaganda efforts had failed to rouse the simple farmers of the river valley. Though the Canadians might wish to believe that the British were about to scatter their families abroad as they had scattered

the Acadians, or even to sell them outright into dread
Spanish slavery, the habitant peasants were not moved to
rebellion. The sowers of seed would not believe the word
of the heretic *Bostonais*, neither the bombast of their government nor the whispering of their sly provocateurs. The
plowmen behind their oxen were as deaf as were their
beasts to the entreaties of the governor general unless, like
the patient animals, they were caught, yoked and put to
the plow.

In their neutrality the habitants of Canada, like the In-
dians, regarded the rebellion as a family affair among the
English. But the Indian was broader in his outlook. In
Canada, he listened to the urging of the Indian agents, and
accepted the king's gifts without committing himself. In
New York Colony, the available leaders of the mighty Six
Nations of the Iroquois came, as though to a party, to a great
council fire that was lighted for them at Albany on 23
August.

General Philip Schuyler made the trip back from Ticonderoga to Albany for the Indian Congress. It had been part
of his charge, as Commander of the Northern Department
of the Army, that he should neutralize the British and Tory
influence over the Indians in the valley west of Albany. As
leader of the invasion army into Canada, General Schuyler
could not move north with hostile Indians threatening his
left flank.

Schuyler was preparing to receive his guests—seven hundred Indian chiefs with their retinues—when George Washington's letter of 20 August was handed to him. The pro-
posal of an overland attack on Quebec City which the

letter contained suggested not only a diversion on Schuyler's right flank, but a demonstration that would draw British troops away from his front. As had been expected of him, General Schuyler wrote at once to General Washington giving his assent to Arnold's expedition. Outside the room in which he wrote, the council was gathering. An arbor had been built to protect the councilors from the August sun. In the center, and open to the stars of the night, the sticks of the council fire were neatly laid. In the fields bordering the Hudson River the noisy life of the Indian camp bustled with preparations to array the chief men for the ceremonial of the council.

His letter to Washington dispatched, Philip Schuyler stood up to buckle on his sword and scabbard. He shrugged into the uniform coat that his aide handed to him and, with hat in hand, stepped out into the day. Schuyler was a frail man, with a mane of fine hair. His grace of movement and his bearing in repose gave credence and authority to the uniform of a major general in the new Continental Army.

Though the Indians at the council were but the residue of the former greatness of the Iroquois League, it was important that Philip Schuyler should treat with them, cajole them, and impress them so that they would live out the summer as neutrals on his exposed flank. Already, the vigor and the strength of the Iroquois had drained off into Canada. The last of it had gone with the exile of the Tory heirs and assigns of the recently deceased Sir William Johnson, baronet of New York. Even now, Carleton was proposing a trip to London for Thayendanegea (Joseph Brandt), in whom the governor recognized the glint of

leadership. That the handsome young Mohawk would be
of a party traveling with Lady Maria Carleton would assure
the Indian of a visit bound to impress him with Britain's
strength.

For days, General Schuyler was trapped with the
shadowy men in the ponderous, sonorous ritual oratory
of the council. Only through patience could he gain the
tenuous peace of Indian neutrality for the duration of his
invasion. Though physically far from well, Philip Schuyler
was forced to sit attentively through all the long sessions,
if he were to serve his distant, waiting army. He could see,
at the edge of the crowd, the messenger down from Ticonderoga with dispatches from Montgomery, but he dared
not move from his seat. He must curb his impatience and
anxiety until all the usages of protocol were exhausted, then
he could accept and read the letter which the man was
now waving in an attempt to catch his eye over the interminable rows of squatting Indians.

Hours later, when Schuyler broke the seal and spread
out Montgomery's letter on the table before him, he learned
that the invasion of Canada had begun without him. Major
John Brown, on yet another secret mission, had written
alarmingly from St. Jean that the new British warships
would soon be ready to take the lake. Faced with this imminent threat of a counter-invasion, Montgomery wrote
that he dared not delay the attack until the general's return,
or even wait for an exchange of letters. Montgomery,
therefore, was taking the army, some guns, and the vessels
down the lake at once, to stopper the British warships in
the narrow reaches of the Richelieu River. A fast whale-

boat was waiting at Ticonderoga to bring the general to his army as soon as the council fire was covered.

* * *

The invasion flotilla left Crown Point early in the day on 30 August 1775. After two days spent in coming down from Ticonderoga in wind and rain, the army was off for Canada with a fair southerly breeze to help it on its way. All hands were in good cheer as they lolled in their various crafts: schooners, sloops, gondolas, bateaux, and whale-boats, while the wind filled the sails.

The Reverend Benjamin Trumbull sat in the most comfortable seat in one of the driest and safest of the better-found vessels of the fleet. From his vantage point he could see the whole expanse of boats, large and small, darting over the water on their reaches and tacks. The fleet was like an eager congregation, hurrying to the parson's church to hear him preach on a clear, blue Sunday morning. There was the text for an exultant sermon in the beauty of the day, the water, the sky, the green shore, and in the rise of the distant mountains to the east. In Canada, whence they marched, prowled the hosts of Midian, arrogant, worldly British to be humbled, painted savages to be scorned, and the abomination of the papacy to be cast into hellfire.

The Reverend Mr. Trumbull was perfectly secure, his meager shanks resting on a folded cloak, his white hands folded in repose on the book on his knee. There was a look of benign condescension and infinite pity on the long face beneath the large, ominously black hat. He was a minister of the cloth in Connecticut, where such things still counted for something, and he was a Trumbull of Connecticut, which counted too. He was sure of his own wisdom in things spiritual and things temporal, and, as he was carried off to war, he was sure of his knowledge of things military.

It was in the purview of his duty to his parishioners, to his colony, and to his family, for the Reverend Benjamin Trumbull to note in his diary and remark in his conversation that the army invading Canada consisted "wholly of Connecticut troops." He did add, however, that of the thousand soldiers in the boats, two hundred—or at the most, two hundred and fifty—of the men, and a few of the officers were from New York. The reverend gentleman was not the first to observe the dearth of natives in the army fighting in and for New York. Colonel Hinman had noticed that, while New York Colony abounded in officers, he had not seen a private. Others commented upon the fact that all of the lucrative jobs in the supply department, as well as the contractors' jobs, were held by Yorkers. Everyone knew that no one was more of an Albany Dutchman than Philip Schuyler, and that the brigadier, riding in his own fast sloop at the head of the flotilla, could also be set down as a New York man.

So the invasion army of Connecticut men went bobbing down the lake with the wind at its back. The calendar month changed while the army was in night camp on shore.

The following morning, Major General Schuyler took his place in the stern of the whaleboat that had waited for him at Ticonderoga. He wrapped his cloak around him against the chill of the first September day. On every side other soldiers were embarking for the trip to Canada. There were artillerymen with their cannon in big bateaux, five hundred men of Hinman's regiment, and three hundred more New Yorkers, the latter being Colonel Goose Van Schaik's regiment, just up from the Hudson. Hurrying on ahead, Schuyler arrived at the foot of Lake Champlain early in the morning on 4 September. The general was stiff and aching as he got out of the boat, and he swayed unsteadily as he stood waiting on the beach. Montgomery, striding down from the camp, saw the fever in the face of his friend and general. Nevertheless, General Schuyler gave the order to move on at once into the Richelieu River. That night, his army around him, the general slept fitfully on Ile aux Noix, halfway to St. Jean.

6

Colonel Arnold Gathers His Men

Ever since he had joined the army to go and fight the red-coats, Caleb Haskell had been standing guards in and around the great camp at Cambridge, Massachusetts. On Saturday night, 10 September 1775, Hunt's company of Moses Little's Newburyport regiment again had the duty on Plowed Hill. From his sentry beat on the southeast slope, Haskell, his iron fife silent in his coat pocket, looked over toward Charlestown Neck and the dark lump of Bunker Hill, where the British were. They had been there since the battle on 17 June. That day had been the only exciting one since Caleb Haskell had come to Cambridge, five months earlier. His fife had given the tune of urgency as the regiment had hurried up to the sound of musket fire on the hill and the thump of cannon from the British ships in the bay. Haskell had run with the rest, with no wind to spare for his fife, when the British had finally carried the crest of the first hill. Since then it had been work, fatigues, guards, and boredom, as the militia companies, reluctantly, had learned discipline. There had been one or two alarms, but they had amounted to nothing but standing around uncomfortably under arms. On occasion, the enemy had bombarded the American camp with cannon balls that, for the most part, rolled harmlessly over the grass. The men gathered them up like eggs from a hayloft. The Indians occasionally went out at night to raid British sentries or to steal horses, or to make other mischief. When the rifle companies came up from Pennsylvania and Virginia to join General Washington's new army, they did this same sneaky work, They, the riflemen from the wild frontier, were like Indians, and in no way did they resemble the good solid townspeople, farmers, and fishermen who made up the bulk of the New England militia. The night raids by the riflemen and the Indians gave Caleb Haskell and his mates something to talk about and, in their boredom, perhaps something to envy.

On Saturday, 9 September, at the regimental muster, Moses Little's regiment was told that orders were out to raise men to go to Canada with Colonel Benedict Arnold. Haskell was a good enough soldier, with enough experience, not to volunteer for anything. But that night he stood guard, was relieved, and was standing guard again when the sun rose over the quiet summit of Bunker Hill. When he came off guard he was warned by his sergeant for fatigue duty. A good soldier, he did his work, not too fast and only well enough to get by. In the afternoon he put his name down to go to Canada. He had done his last guard on Plowed Hill, drawn his last fatigue from the sergeant of Captain Hunt's company, stood his last regimental muster for Colonel Little; to get away from Cambridge, he had even volunteered.

Caleb Haskell was not alone in his restless desire to go where there was a chance to do what he had joined the army for: to fight the ministerial troops. Seven hundred and forty-seven other New England militiamen answered Adjutant General Horatio Gates's call for volunteers to go with Arnold. According to camp gossip, Benedict Arnold was one to go looking for a fight.

Some did not volunteer of their own accord. There was a fine fight over on Winter Hill on the morning of 8 September, and because he had started it, Private Kimball and his mate were dragged off to the guardhouse. Fifteen minutes later, the lieutenant came storming into the room where the battered instigators lay, dabbing at their cuts and scratches with filthy handkerchiefs. When the lieutenant left, Kimball and his friend left with him. They stopped briefly at the hut they had wrecked, where the two privates picked up their muskets and their few belongings. From Winter Hill, the two were marched to Cambridge, where the lieutenant saw them duly "volunteered" into Captain Henry Dearborn's company of Colonel Arnold's expeditionary force.

So they came, the men of the four New England colonies, each under a different set of circumstances, to pass before the mustering officer. Across his little table, the adjutant general's man scrutinized each volunteer, looking for the young, the strong, the active. Through perfunctory questions, most of which were not truthfully answered, he sought those men familiar with the woods and those experienced in handling a bateau in white water. The lucky ones were the convincing ones. They had their names written down in one of the ten musket companies whose rolls were the volunteers' passport out of the inert boredom, the repressive inaction, of the great sprawling camp of General Washington's army at Cambridge.

If the private soldier who volunteered to march with Arnold to Quebec was motivated by a desire to "get mowing" in the fields of war, so was the officer who was put over him. His route to active service, too, was through the office of the adjutant general. As Arnold himself had done in May, and as the enlisted man was doing, the officer had to shuck himself from the local militia company with which he had come to Cambridge. His way was made easy by the authorized open recruiting into the Continental Army. Once commissioned, the officer eager to join Benedict Arnold's bold venture found many ways to achieve the preferred assignment: Christopher Greene found it helpful to be a relative of Brigadier General Nathanael Greene. Arnold was happy to have the well-placed thirty-eight-year-old Rhode Island gentleman as one of his two division commanders. The other lieutenant colonel, Roger Enos, had pretenses of being an experienced soldier. He had served in Connecticut's army in the French War, in Canada, in the west, and in the West Indies, presumably acquiring a knowledge of the administration and movement of supplies. With this reputation and with his seniority in age —at forty-six he was the gaffer of the army—Enos earned the command of the rear of the column of march, where the bulk supplies moved forward at a more leisurely pace over tried ways.

Neither of Arnold's two majors was distinguished by a flagrant personality. Timothy Bigelow was a Worcester blacksmith. He owed his commission to George Washington, who had noticed the discipline that the big blacksmith had bellows-blown and anvil-hammered into his company of militiamen. Return Jonathan Meigs was a steady man, as became a merchant of Connecticut. He honored his father, wrote frequent letters to his wife, remembered those who were kind, and listened with a closed mouth.

In the society of the armies, there is no greater trust or responsibility than that which devolves upon the company officer. He stands next to the common soldier. On him, the whole hierarchy of command relies to take that first step forward that leads so quickly on to the last step in life. In the grand schemes of government, the company officer risks not nations nor cities nor cyphered soldiers, but his intimates. He recognizes the man by the character of his walk or the way he habitually wears the hat. In the quiet moments of leisure, he has heard the man's hopes and his jokes. When face to face on a matter of discipline, the company officer listens to the soldier's excuse and judges the man. There are many points of intimacy in company life where the man and the officer assess each other's strength and weakness. When, in war, the time comes to move forward into the open, the company officer risks his life on his own conviction; the common soldier follows in reliance on the officer over him.

Ten company captains were qualified and chosen to

lead the volunteers on the march to Quebec. Some had fought the French in the old war, some had withstood the British volleys and turned back the bayonet charge on Bunker Hill, and some had strong political credentials. Among the latter was nineteen-year-old Captain Samuel Ward, who was not found wanting, despite the fact that his father had twice been governor of Rhode Island. At the first shot at Lexington, Henry Dearborn gave up the study of medicine to "go for a soldier." His captain's commission under Benedict Arnold was a first step toward greatness. William Goodrich, a forest man close to Indians and their way of life, found himself captain of a company of volunteers from Maine. Captain Simeon Thayer was a quiet-living wig-maker. In his past he had survived the awful siege and massacre at Fort William Henry, and had served with the terrible rangers of the great Major Robert Rogers. First favorite among Colonel Arnold's volunteer captains was the moody Oliver Hanchet. Williams, Scott, Topham and McCobb were other captains who, in the staging camp at Cambridge, faced for the first time the men they were to lead on the long march to the distant battleground.

In his wisdom, General Washington had assigned three companies of riflemen to complete Colonel Arnold's army, and to complement the *ad hoc* units of volunteers. These were the companies from the western frontier, where the stockaded fort and not the tall white steeple was the focal point of community life. The riflemen were a kindred type, bound together by the mutual usages of the frontier, each man wedded to his cherished rifle, which was sister

to every other rifle. In their long march out of the wide
frontier onto the crowded coastal land, the western men,
compressed by the unfamiliar, became tight units under
their respective officers. Through the tiny villages and close
countryside of New England, they walked loosely, heads
turning, eyes searching as in a strange forest. Trained and
accomplished in their own work, there were few jobs and
much mischief for the rifle companies in the camp at
Cambridge.

It was rumored among the New England troops that,
when the call had gone out for three companies to go with
Arnold, the officers of these strangers gambled with dice for
the privilege of being chosen. The choice, however made,
fell on two companies from Pennsylvania and a company
from Washington's native Virginia. Of these, Captain Daniel Morgan, the Virginian, was the undoubted leader.

In the summer of 1755, Colonel George Washington,
riding in the splendor of General Edward Braddock's staff,
would have taken scant notice of a boy drover, braking his
wagon down the western slopes of the Allegheny Mountains, on the British march toward Pittsburgh. In the disaster that befell Braddock's army, the young colonel from
Virginia could easily have forgotten that a boy drover was
given five hundred lashes for presuming to strike a British
officer. But Daniel Morgan never forgot that flogging.
Whenever he pulled off his fringed hunting shirt, exposing
his broad back and massive shoulders, the welts were there
for all to see. He invited the curious to count the stripes
and tell him if Justice had not indeed miscarried, and there
were but four hundred and ninety-nine.

Captain Daniel Morgan was thirty-nine years old when he marched his company of riflemen from Virginia to give back to the British that last forgotten blow. The near-white woods clothes that he wore as a uniform added the appearance of bulk to Morgan's imposing two-hundred-pound weight and his six feet of height. His voice was strong rather than loud, which made everyone heed the decisive orders that he gave, irrespective of his authority to give them. But it was Daniel Morgan's enduring stamina —four hundred and ninety-nine lashes worth—that assured the acceptance of his natural leadership.

On 11 September, being ready, packed, and waiting, Arnold's three rifle companies left Cambridge on the first stage of the march to Quebec. After the first halt to rest and to adjust packs and straps, Captains Smith and Hendricks came to the head of the column to walk awhile with Daniel Morgan. For the two hundred and fifty route-wise riflemen, the two-day, fifty-mile march to Newbury-port was but a Sunday stroll to the well where the girls would be. In the clear air, free from the churned-up dust, William Hendricks walked quietly beside Morgan over the rolling hills. Back in his company at the very tail of the line, Sergeant Joseph Greer trudged along, at his side the big, strong woman he had married. Captain Hendricks would see to it that later on in the march the companies would take turn and turn about at leading down the dusty road. Ambling along on the far side of Daniel Morgan was Captain Mathew Smith. For over ten years, he had been the military and revolutionary leader of Lancaster County in Pennsylvania. With the Paxton Boys, he had killed In-

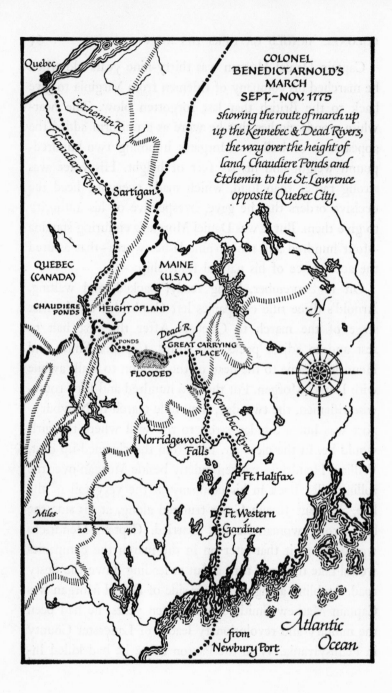

COLONEL
BENEDICT ARNOLD'S
MARCH
SEPT. – NOV. 1775

showing the route of march up
up the Kennebec & Dead Rivers,
the way over the height of
land, Chaudiere Ponds and
Etchemin to the St. Lawrence
opposite Quebec City.

Quebec

Etchemin R.

Chaudiere River

Sartigan

QUEBEC
(CANADA)

MAINE
(U.S.A.)

CHAUDIERE
PONDS

HEIGHT OF LAND

Dead R.

PONDS

GREAT CARRYING
PLACE

FLOODED

N

Kennebec River

Norridgewock
Falls

Ft. Halifax

Miles

0   20   40

Ft. Western
Gardiner

Atlantic
Ocean

from
Newbury Port

dians when and where he could find them, using such ingenious methods that he was abhorred in Philadelphia. Where Mathew Smith went he trailed, like smoke from a sugarhouse chimney, the smell of good Pennsylvania whiskey. While Smith was up front with the other captains, Lieutenant Archibald Steele, the scout, led the men of Lancaster. Keeping pace with the lieutenant's easy stride was sixteen-year-old John Joseph Henry. His father, a gunsmith, had entrusted the boy as a cadet to the company, so many of whom bought their fitted rifles from him.

The departure of the musket companies from Cambridge was delayed until almost the middle of September. As in a new gristmill, last minute adjustments must be made in a new army, until the big wheel turning in the stream can be thrown in, and the gears, groaning and protesting, can turn to the purpose for which they have been assembled. Some of the companies had not drawn all their cold weather clothing. In some, the lieutenants had gone to fetch in the last of the volunteers, to bring their strength up to the establishment of eighty-four. In Captain Scott's company of Colonel Enos's division, the men refused to march until they had been paid. On 13 September, a Wednesday, all things having been resolved, the ten companies set out independently for Newburyport, where transports had been assembled to take them on up the coast. Sergeant John Pierce, a surveyor, mapped the taverns and the girls along the route, and in his new guise of savior and hero, found lavish hospitality which he willingly accepted.

For two days after the last man left, Colonel Arnold stayed in Cambridge, doing the final staff work. Early on

Friday morning, the horses were saddled, ready, and waiting at the door. With his small staff and the grooms, Arnold mounted and rode out through the big camp, just rousing itself for yet another day of drill, duty, and discipline.

Eleazar Oswald was with his colonel as confidential secretary, as he had been on Lake Champlain. Christian Febiger rode with them as brigade major. Arnold had known Febiger's father in the Danish West Indies, and when the young Dane had turned up, involved in the army of the rebellion, Colonel Arnold had taken him into his official family as a likely, educated, intelligent aide. The other members of the headquarters detachment were somewhere ahead with the troops, supposedly doing their specialized duties. But Dr. Isaac Senter and his mate trudged the rutted miles on aching feet, bantering the simples of sympathy with other soldiers as they came up with them. Samuel Spring, wandering along in his black canonicals, did not look like the backwoods chaplain he would so soon become. With him walked his fellow graduate of Princeton College, the diminutive little rooster Aaron Burr.

Colonel Arnold's party broke the journey to dine in Salem. Oswald ate quickly, as he had to arrange the transport of two hundred and seventy blankets, awaiting the army in the government stores in Salem. As they remounted, Oswald could report to his colonel that he had procured two hundred pounds of medicinal ginger, to spice the food and help the dyspepsia in the days ahead. It was ten o'clock at night when the command party finally dismounted outside the lighted house of Nathaniel Tracy in Newburyport. Before he finally went to bed, Benedict Arnold walked out to look toward the harbor where his eleven transports rode the mooring-lines silently in the darkness. In the morning, the colonel would send three of the fastest vessels up the coast and seaward from the Isle of Shoals, to see if the British waited there. There was no doubt that General Gage in Boston knew of the expedition. If there had been time to organize it, and if frigates were available, Arnold could expect an attack from the British Navy on this short sea leg of the journey to Quebec.

Until the picket boats returned and the contrary wind shifted, the whole army must wait in port. It was not until Monday, 18 September, that, all things being favorable, the transports sailed away as a fleet.

7

The Kennebec

Colonel Benedict Arnold left his flagship while she rode at anchor in Merry Meeting Bay. He had been aboard her for almost three whole days, and had done all the work that Oswald had found for him in the field desk. Letters had been written, reports checked over, lists of supplies tabulated, men assigned and reassigned. Arnold, the commander, could no longer wait on the shift of the wind and the turn of the tide. His work was up ahead, at Reuben Colburn's place at Gardinerstown on the Kennebec. There the bateaux that Colburn had been commissioned to build were, or should be, ready. The scout of local men that Colburn had been asked to send should be back with news of discoveries on the upper rivers and over the Height of Land. The rowing-boat in which Arnold now rode took him into the mouth proper of the Kennebec River. There was a squawking, and a movement of migrant ducks in the marshes at the lower end of Swan Island. High above the tall-reaching pines of the mainland, a ragged gaggle of geese was struggling into its V, to ride the northwest wind southward. A crook-necked crane flapped lazily over the boat, its long black legs behind it. The vessels of the invasion fleet lay far astern, their bows, contrary to the autumn life of the bay and river, pointing to the north.

The men of Arnold's army rested in the transports most of the day of 21 September. Many of the riflemen, accustomed only to the rolling, cresting mountains of the Alleghenies, had felt the qualms of seasickness from the moment they dropped their packs on the uncertain decks of the transports in Newburyport Harbor. The rest of the landsmen were moaning and retching at the first dip of the bows into the rolling Atlantic swells beyond Plum Island. A boisterous wind had buffeted the boats all the way down the coasts of Massachusetts, New Hampshire, and Maine. A thick wet fog had blanketed the fleet when it entered the passage in behind Sequin Island, where the sea lane turned inland. Health returned quickly to the soldiers with the sight and smell of the land, which was now a sleeve fitted closely to the water-course leading up into Merry Meeting Bay. A spirit of competition developed as the soldiers at the sweeps made a race of their rowing up the narrow passage. Jeers greeted the vessels that ran aground on the edges of the channel. Under the roaring voice of the mate, Ephraim Squires grumbled as he toiled to free the stranded schooner *Hannah*. His journey and that of his company (the men who, back in Cambridge, had demanded their pay) had been particularly bad. They had been aboard the *Swallow* when she ran aground in Newburyport harbor. With the others of Captain Scott's Company, Squires had been dumped on the deck of the already crowded *Hannah*. Now she, the "contrary old sow," had found her own mudbank in which to wallow in this sty of a river.

One of the first three transports to arrive off Gardinerstown was the *Betsy*, with Captain Jonas Hubbard's company on board. At her quarterdeck rail, Sergeant and Engineer John Pierce looked over at the neat town, proudly flaunting its Liberty Pole. What held his eye, and the eyes of all on board, were the rows and rows of bateaux lined up on the shore. They were small craft, these river wagons, flat-bottomed, double-ended, and made of newly sawed evergreen boards. They should have been moored in the water, soaking up their caulked seams. Each bateau would take its load of barrels and kegs and the men to row, paddle or pole it, up the shallow rapids and against the clear-flowing current of the quiet reaches of the river. The men of the companies, walking along the shore, would man-handle their bateaux and cargo around the high falls and over the long portage across the Height of Land that lay ahead.

The bateaumen of Hubbard's company were climbing down the sides of the *Betsy* to row ashore and draw their bateaux from the yard. Arnold himself was on the foreshore to greet the soldiers. Through cupped hands, he shouted across to the *Betsy*'s Captain to get on upriver to Fort Weston, where the stores would be off-loaded and the soldiers set ashore. Pierce stayed on deck, watching the river with a surveyor's eye until after six o'clock, when the rain began to fall and the *Betsy* anchored.

The captain and his crew gave a farewell dinner of roast beef in the cabin, a dinner to which Sergeant Pierce was invited. Later, when the rain stopped, Captain Hubbard, with his lieutenant and Pierce, went on shore to sleep in real beds. It was a memorable last night of comfort for the sergeant-surveyor. Within thirty-six hours Pierce was in a bateau being rowed upstream, his journey to Quebec begun.

There were nineteen men in the two groups that set out together in the rain of that Sunday afternoon, 24 September. Pierce was of the survey party. He rode with a compass in his hand and, on his knee, a notebook in which he entered the bearings of the river, ticked off the miles of open water, measured and marked the portage tracks, and entered descriptions of all the rapids and falls. The survey party's main work, ahead of the army, was to pioneer the Great Carrying Place, which Montresor had described in his journal and which the Indians tried to conceal. Eighty-four river miles from Fort Weston, the way to the Height of Land left the Kennebec at the outlet of a brook. The blazed trail climbed up a steep hill to a plateau on which were three ponds capable of floating the army's bateaux. Beyond the third lake and over a low saddle, the portage trail dropped down to the west branch of the Kennebec River, called the Dead River. The Great Carry, fourteen miles from beaching to launching, saved many weary, nearly impossible miles of river travel. The Great Carry was expected to be the most rigorous part of the whole long road to Quebec.

With work to do along the way, the survey party in their bateau soon fell behind the other group that had set out with them on that Sunday afternoon. Lieutenant Archibald

Steele, with ten men, was traveling light, fast and far in two birchbark canoes. Steele's was a long-range reconnaissance patrol that had little time to waste on the Kennebec. Their work began beyond the Great Carrying Place and continued to the source of the Chaudière, over the Height of Land. The nine riflemen and their two canoemen-guides also had a security mission to perform. They were under orders to capture or kill the Indian Natanis, who lived alone in the only cabin on two hundred miles of the road. Natanis was reported to be a "Great Spy" for the British.

Colonel Arnold sent out Lieutenant Steele's scout to corroborate a preliminary scout that somehow had failed. When he was first planning the expedition in Cambridge, Arnold had asked Reuben Colburn to hire woodsmen to make a reconnaissance of the route. Colburn had sent Jeremiah Getchel of Vassalboro, in Maine, with three friends, and supplies bought on the army's account.

With a copy of that account on his desk, Arnold had interviewed Getchel on his arrival at Fort Weston, eight miles above Gardinerstown. On interrogation, the forest man admitted that he had gone no farther than the Great Carry—the other side of the Great Carry. Getchel claimed that there had been no need to go farther; in fact, to do so would have endangered the whole scouting expedition. An Indian woman whom they met had told them that the British had put savage Mohawks from New York into the woods above the town of Sartigan. Getchel, too, had seen and talked to the Abenaki Natanis, who was a "Great Spy," of course, and not to be trusted. Natanis had not told him of the Mohawks, only that an officer and six redcoats dwelt in a house in Sartigan.

To counterbalance the veracity of Getchel's report, Arnold had the man's account-claim against the army. On it, the item "six gallons of rhum" loomed large. That was a quantity to stir the imagination and to prompt four men more to serious drinking than to arduous travel. So Arnold had strengthened Steele's patrol with reliable riflemen. To give the man a second chance, he sent Getchel along as guide; to avoid any risk, he ordered the removal of Natanis.

When the two advance parties had gone, the colonel gave his full attention to the army. On Monday, he sent the three rifle companies forward with forty-five days' provisions in their bateaux. They drew axes to clear and widen the road over the Great Carry. The next day, Lieutenant Colonel Greene embarked his division and set out upstream. At noon on 27 September, Major Meigs moved out with his four companies. Private James Melvin of Dearborn's company, Meigs's division, spent most of 28 September knee-deep, sometimes thigh-deep, in the water, wrestling his bateau through the ripples and swift current of the river. Melvin and the men of the division spent a cold night in wet clothes, in bivouac all along the river. The next day they came to the first portage road across from Fort Halifax, and got their bateaux over it.

Colonel Arnold overtook Dearborn's and Goodrich's companies there. He had stayed at Fort Weston to be with Lieutenant Colonel Enos, who was loading stores into the last of the bateaux. Some of the boats, knocked together in a hurry, needed last-minute patching. At Fort Weston,

Arnold finished the staff work that still tied him to the army
at Cambridge. An officer from General Washington's staff
was waiting to take back the last reports, dispatches, and
requests. There were still supplies to come up from the
transports at Gardinerstown. There was a residue of punishment to be meted out in the interest of discipline and
control. Three men were whipped, and another, of Captain
Scott's company, was whipped and drummed out of camp
in disgrace for stealing. A sergeant was publicly stripped of
his rank, and there was one man to be hanged. Arnold saw
it in his heart, and for the good of morale, to reprieve
the latter, a simple Irishman with homicidal temper when
drunk. The wretch, with the halter still about his neck,
was led back down from the stage while the soldiers of
Enos's division looked on in silent awe.

At Fort Weston, too, Arnold gave a last look over his
shoulder toward his home in New Haven. He wrote to
his sister Hannah, who was caring for his motherless children. In the written orders that he left with Colonel Enos,
he set the rendezvous for Chaudière Pond. All that work
being done, Benedict Arnold set out to lead his army from
in front.

Traveling in a dugout canoe (the one of birch bark in
which he had started proved leaky and wet), Colonel
Arnold overtook the companies, one by one. On the night
of 1 October he lodged at the Widow Warren's house.
The next day he left behind the last English settlement,
at Skowhegan Falls. His hired Indian paddlers moved the
light craft swiftly up the next five-mile reach of the river.
They passed through Greene's division. The men in the

bateaux and the little groups making their way along the shore waved and called out greeting to the colonel as he passed by.

Arnold went ashore at the landing place below the elbow gorge through which the Kennebec tumbles in a cascade of white water. The place was called Norridgewock by the tribe of Abenakis who, until recently, had lived there in a village now razed by the colonials. Walking up the portage road, Arnold passed by the ruins of their Romish church and the place where their last French priest, killed by the British, lay under a stone cross. The whole place was a memorial and a lesson to the Canadians that Massachusetts Protestants would not tolerate Papist trespass on their lands.

Colonel Arnold was across the portage in time to see Morgan and the "Riflers" re-embark. They were big men, spruce and easy in their uniform hunting shirts. They were familiar in the handling of their boats. The walking parties seemed to be ambling toward the woods, into which they disappeared, noiselessly, without a trace, like an otter into its pool.

For the next eight days, Arnold remained at the Norridgewock portage. When he returned to the landing site after seeing the riflemen away, he found Captains Thayer and Hubbard waiting for him. They had their barrels open, the contents tipped out onto blankets spread on the grass. One look into the yawning round mouths at the dirty mass of dough in the bottom of the barrels told the story of leakage and spoilage. There was a beginning of the gray whiskers of mold.

Hubbard and Thayer, like anxious house dogs who had been misunderstood, hovered around Arnold as he strode down to the beach. Eagerly they showed him the bateaux. On this one a floorboard had been carelessly nailed; on that one a hardwood knee had cracked on a knot that should not have been there; most of the bateaux showed signs of patchy recaulking, done at the last carry. Both captains cursed the slipshod work of the greedy contractors.

The reason for the damage to the precious, carefully measured food lay as much in the ineptitude of the patient private soldier in dealing with the river as in the avarice of Contractor Colburn. If blame were to be apportioned, however, it must also be shared with the mustermaster back in Cambridge. He had accepted the eager plowboy as an experienced bateauman. Equipped only with an innocent devotion to duty, to get that bateau up and over the rises and the treads of the river, the soldier attacked his laden vessel. Too often, the boy who humped grain sacks with ease in his father's mill misjudged the angle and the place to set the pole that held his bateau bows into the current. As the bateau yawed and the youth sought to avert disaster, the river came in and sloshed in the bottom of the boat. There the water lay, seeping into the barrels where the biscuits and pork were tightly packed.

At Skowhegan Falls, Abner Stocking of Connecticut stood with his mates of Hanchet's company, looking up through a fissure to the top of the cliff, a hundred feet above. In the next few minutes, they would haul, push, and scramble their bateau to the top. On several previous trips up the fissure, Stocking had carried his equipment, his share of oars, paddles, poles, and his weight of barrels. The bateau was leaking badly as they rowed upriver to the next carry, at Norridgewock.

Arnold was there when Stocking arrived. He helped haul the boat to shore. Captain Hanchet was there, too, as the men off-loaded the barrels and opened them for inspection. There was more moldy bread to strike from the strength of the army stores.

Major Meigs had also met with disaster. Just before Norridgewock his bateau had begun to founder. His buckskin breeches were sodden, and water still poured from the long tails of his uniform coat when he presented himself to Colonel Arnold. In the mishap, Meigs had lost his camp kettle, in which he had stored the meaningful luxuries of a lump of butter and a loaf of sugar.

In spite of the loss of critical foods, Colonel Arnold kept the companies moving forward. There was a delay at Norridgewock carrying place while the company of carpenters, which Arnold's foresight had provided for, patched the battered boats and recoopered sprung barrels. When Colonel Enos came up with the rearguard, Arnold himself was ready to go again to the head of the column. A storm of rain held him back in the tent for one more restless day. On 10 October, while weaving through a myriad of small islands, Arnold first noticed that the mountains were closing in on the river. The rain of two days before had fallen as snow in the higher elevations. The summits, humps, and ridges were all white and glistening in the bright sunshine.

There was no need for the colonel to look out for the natural marks—a sugarloaf mountain, sharp eastward bend in the river—to find the beginning of the Great Carrying Place. Bateaux of the army nuzzled the shore on both sides of the brook, like piglets at a sow. Arnold was impressed by the size of the brook that came out of the first pond on the high ground above. Leaping from his dugout canoe the moment she touched, he forged up the road. At the top of the ridge he paused to watch the line of heavily burdened soldiers pass by. They were winded from the climb and they looked tired, but they were cheerful. When Febiger and Oswald, with the colonel's ever-present field desk, caught up with him, the three walked on together. They caught a ride over the first pond, where men were fishing and catching trout for the evening meal. Across the second pond Arnold chose a spot and they set up headquarters.

There Dr. Senter found him. Captain Williams, at the rear of the army, was recovering from his dysentery but was still so weak that he could scarcely walk, much less command his company. Ten or twelve men were nearly played out, and in the surgeon's opinion, could not go on. He proposed building a hospital, a log shelter, and leaving the most seriously incapacitated of the men there, to recover and go back. Arnold agreed, and detailed Captain Goodrich's company to build a hut of logs. The place chosen was between the first and second ponds, where Ensign Irvin now lay helpless, his joints swollen and stiffened by rheumatism. Arnold had seen the stricken officer, and had given an encouraging word to him. Four riflemen attended Irvin, keeping a fire, feeding him, turning the helpless man, even brushing flies from the sweat of pain and weakness on his brow. Obviously, four good men needed

at Quebec could not be left behind to care for one sick
officer, so in Arnold's hospital the sick would care for each
other, and the sickest, Irvin, would be in charge. He had
been trained in Philadelphia as a doctor.

Dr. Senter was still at Arnold's camp when Lieutenant
Steele came in, wood-stained and tired almost beyond hunger. His scout had been to the Height of Land, and from
the top of a tall tree he had seen the long bright finger of
Chaudière Pond glistening on the plain. The men had also
seen the smoke of Indian campfires in that wilderness, but
whether they were the fires of friendly Abenakis from
Maine or those of the Mohawks, Steele did not risk his
mission to find out. The scout had returned, making cold
fireless camps each night, and not daring to shoot the game
that abounded along the Dead River, lest the unseen Indians
should be hostile. Steele had left his exhausted men resting
at the far end of the Great Carry, where Morgan's men
would find them and bring food. Lieutenant Steele himself was hungry. No, they had not caught Natanis. They
had rushed in from all sides on his cabin, but the false Indian had fled.

As the lieutenant was eating, Colonel Arnold outlined the
next job that he had for the scout. Again, with the survey
party, Steele was to go ranging far ahead of the army. The
survey party was to mark well the trail to the Chaudière
Pond. The scouts were to try the Chaudière River down to,
but not into, the first Canadian settlement. As soon as he had
finished his meal, Lieutenant Steele set out, walking briskly,
with a new purpose. Those at the headquarters fire saw
him turn into the portage road, where a bateau carried by

four men was just passing on its way over to the third pond. Lightly, the lieutenant from Pennsylvania stepped under the overturned boat, and they saw him take the weight of it from a shoulder of one of the men.

In the days he spent at his forest headquarters, Colonel Arnold saw his key officers. They talked of Quebec, and they talked of soon meeting Major General Schuyler's Northern Army there, on the Plains of Abraham. By the light of the fire, warmed by a measure of rum, they counted eight or ten days to the Chaudière Pond. The twenty-five days of rations would easily take them all the way to Quebec, or at worst, into the inhabited lands where food could be bought. All the officers acknowledged that the journey up the swiftly flowing Kennebec had been far worse than they had expected. Those officers who had been to the Dead River assured the others that it was indeed placid, dead. From the rough census taken at the bivouac beside the portage road, Arnold figured that he now had nine-hundred-and-fifty effective men in his army.

When at night the camp grew quiet, Benedict Arnold got out his field desk and wrote his letters. One he wrote to General Washington, to report his progress and set down his expectations. One went to John Manir, Esquire, in Quebec City. To this Friend of Liberty, Arnold wrote that he was coming with two thousand soldiers, and asked for the military and civil news out of Quebec. The letter to Manir was to be delivered by Eneas, an Indian in whose fidelity Arnold placed full trust. Another letter, also carried by Eneas, was addressed to "The Honorable Major General and Commander of the Northern Army." In this letter to

Schuyler, Colonel Arnold set the rendezvous at Quebec City for a fortnight hence. The two letters going north were deceptively marked as written "On the Dead River, 160 miles from Quebec." They were dated correctly, "Oct. 13, 1775."

8

"The Privates are all Generals"

Major General Philip Schuyler was no longer in Canada with the field force of his northern command. The illness that he had resisted for so long eventually came upon him with such severity that he had to give in to it. He scarcely protested as they laid him down in a covered boat, and on the morning of 16 September he began the long journey from Ile aux Noix to Ticonderoga. Mrs. Schuyler had been summoned, and arrived at the old French fort shortly after the general himself. Without stopping to change her stained and rumpled traveling clothes, Catherine Schuyler swept into the sickroom. She changed the bed, built up the fire, and bathed her husband. She gave him a fresh nightshirt and, with an arm around his shoulders, made him sip the evil-tasting medicine which she concocted from the contents of her bottle-box. Under his wife's care, the general's fever subsided and the taste of bile left his mouth. With the end of physical torment, the trial of General Schuyler's patience began.

A still bright autumn day, with a warm sun high in the

sky, gave the recuperating general a chance to walk out on the curtain wall of the fort. Through an empty gun embrasure, Schuyler could look down on the lake shore, where military stores awaited transshipment to the army in Canada. Two large bateaux, one of them partially loaded, were tied up at the dock, their crews mingling where a man was fishing from his seat on a bollard. A small bateau with a light cargo of powder kegs was coming in to land. She was from the Lake George end of the road that funneled through the post at Ticonderoga. The boxes, barrels, kegs, and cases, few enough in number, were dumped haphazardly on the trampled grass. Amidst the untidy litter the soldiers slouched about their tasks, unsupervised and seemingly careless of their comrades who were in contact with a shooting enemy just ahead. Though these idle, indolent men were the culls of the garrison that Montgomery had taken north, they were healthy enough to hump the cargoes forward. They needed only the animation which the convalescing general was about to give them.

A few sharp inquiries told Philip Schuyler that the stagnation apparent at Fort Ti reached far back down the line. At Lake George, barrels of perishable food lay uncovered on the damp ground, exposed to the weather. A bateau, loaded with mortar bombs, had been sunk in the lake. At Albany, Brigadier General David Wooster, the venerable veteran, was dawdling along northward with additional Connecticut troops. He had paused in the city to stage a handsome military display for the people of Albany. The general and his official guests were agreed that the troops did the slow step as gracefully as regulars, and were a credit

to Connecticut. Specific orders sent back to Wooster
brought him ponderously on toward Canada.

In spite of his weakness and over the protests of his wife,
Schuyler abruptly brought his convalescence to an end, to
become the commander in chief of the Northern Department of the Continental Army. As such, Philip Schuyler
was the linchpin holding and joining the cumbersome supply wagon to Montgomery's team, plodding the Canadian
roads to victory. General Schuyler fitted himself into his
assumed position with an energy that brought forth effi-
ciency. To the problems of procurement and delivery,
Schuyler applied the sound business practices of the man
of affairs that he had been before becoming a soldier.
Toward the laggards he bent all the fury of his aristocratic
imperiousness. Tact and charm without weakness gained
Schuyler the co-operation of those officers of the Northern
Army who, by virtue of rank, considered themselves his
equal. Only to George Washington, his acknowledged superior, did Schuyler report truly of the discouragement he
often felt. With Catherine, his wife, Philip Schuyler shared
a sustaining patriotic zeal for the rebel cause.

Brigadier General Richard Montgomery, who once had
borrowed Schuyler's army, was in close accord with his
commander. When illness removed Schuyler from the
field, Montgomery was the troop commander in whom
the general reposed trust with confidence, and reliance
without doubt. At his post of danger, where artillery shells
fell in anger and the enemy did the unexpected, Montgomery received the men and matériel which were the
product of Schuyler's organization in the army's rear. That

the problems of the army, too, came forward with the rations was but a shared part of Brigadier General Montgomery's job in gaining the tactical victory to attain Major General Schuyler's strategic objective.

Some of the difficulties had manifested themselves during the twelve days that General Schuyler had commanded the army in the field. Although Montgomery had taken the army north without orders, he had not had to make the initial invasion of Canadian soil alone. Philip Schuyler was in the command boat when, on 4 September, the army of nine hundred men glided down the Richelieu River to land before dark on Ile aux Noix. All was quiet on the river. The dreaded British schooner had not come out to protest their trespass.

On 6 September, General Schuyler had wished to try the British defenses at St. Jean and test the loyalty of the Canadians whom he had invited to join him. A mile above the fort, the command boat had turned in to shore, and the troop boats had wheeled left to their landings on the west shore. Forming up quickly, the soldiers marched off by companies toward the fort, which, at that distance, appeared to be a line of raw earth, a roof, and a flagpole showing above. The head of the marching column scarcely had found its pace when the two leading companies sprang the ambush. For half an hour, the two companies pressed the enemy back through the forest fringe and into the swampy land, where they vanished among the cattails. Leaning heavily on a stick, a musket ball in the muscle of his thigh, Major Thomas Hobby brought his command back to the army. Behind the major came the other com-

pany commander, borne on a rude stretcher. At the back
of the straggling line of elated troops, three gray-faced
wounded men were carried; with them were five Connecticut dead.

Quietly, remembering the limpness of the recent dead,
the troops unslung their shovels and set to raising a breastwork. Their work was not unnoticed by the British in the
fort. A few ranging shells thudded into the ground
near the diggers, or plopped into the river where the boats
were drawn up. As the sun went down, the cannonading
increased, and Schuyler ordered the men's work abandoned for a new position, three-quarters of a mile away.
Grudgingly, wearily, the Connecticut men shouldered
their tools, picked up their muskets, their coats, and their
equipment and tagged along into the gloom behind their
New York general.

Late that night, a low hail from the river brought a
muffled spy to shore for a secret meeting alone with General Schuyler in his tent. The shadow man was as convincing as he was depressing. The new fort at St. Jean, he
reported, was strong of wall and amply supplied with
cannon and defenders. The new schooner, *Royal Savage*,
carried sixteen guns and was ready. The worst news that
the spy had to impart was the fact that the Canadians
would not join the Americans. What the Connecticut
troops boasted of as "Major Hobby's victory" was, to the
Canadians, a defeat. In the action of 6 September, sixty
Indians led by a New York tory refugee had stopped a
whole army of "fifteen hundred" timid *Bostonais*. Before

going back to the river from whence he had come, the midnight spy urged Schuyler to return to Ile aux Noix.

After conferring with his officers the next morning, Schuyler took the spy's advice. Again, the Connecticut troops left the work they had been doing to move back and begin yet another piece of defensive work on Ile aux Noix. General Schuyler found it necessary to write an explanatory order for the move; the Connecticut men, from generals to privates, were accustomed to debate "publick affaires."

While they worked and pondered and sought advice from their clergy, their army was reinforced. Four hundred NewYorkers of Colonel Goose Van Schaick's 2nd New York Regiment arrived, and, to keep the voting majority, there came three hundred more Connecticut men. Most welcome of the new arrivals was Captain John Lamb's New York Artillery Company, with guns and mortars. These last, General Montgomery hurried into position to cover the defensive boom that blocked the passage down each side of the island.

Into the tangling rivalries of the crowded little island in the Richelieu River came new intelligence from the Canadian communities downriver. Schuyler had sent John Brown and Ethan Allen, now acting in a private capacity, on a contact mission into Canada. From James Livingston, a Chambly merchant related to Montgomery's wife, came a letter that cast doubt on all the information the spy had whispered to the general. Livingston promised a "considerable party" of Canadians if Schuyler would but interpose a force between St. Jean and Chambly.

On 10 September, General Schuyler made the attempt to infiltrate beyond the British fort. The operation, the general's last before going sick, was a complete shambles. The New York troops, who were to march by night around the west side of St. Jean, panicked. Most of the men were idlers, scavenged from the alleys of the city. Though hardy enough in the shadow jungle of the street, they were terrified by the silence and by the sounds of the forest at night. They were frightened, too, of the Indians. With the strange muskets that the army had given them, they nervously fired at each other as they moved through the darkness. They wandered among the trees and lost their bearings. Then, overcome by their own fears, all five hundred of them stampeded for the river. In their headlong flight from the forest, they collided with the covering party of Connecticut troops that Montgomery had set up in the fieldworks built on the 6 September.

Though the brigadier attempted to calm and quiet the demoralized men, in the face of new rumors he could not hold them on the river position. The fear of Indians in the night became, with the day, a dread of the *Royal Savage*. The schooner, its guns run out, would come—was coming now! There was a rush to get away, and it was only under a semblance of leadership that Montgomery and his officers led the troops back to Ile aux Noix.

The Connecticut troops on the island turned out to jeer and sneer at the timid Yorkers as they came ashore. That the only success of the expedition was a Connecticut one, added to the arrogant confidence of the New

Englanders. One of the gunboats had hit and sunk a British gunboat that had come snooping upriver.

Montgomery watched the covered boat make the short tack over to the east shore of the Richelieu River. Though Ethan Allen had assured him that all of the British Indians had gone home, there was always the chance that some of them had stayed to prowl. The boat bearing the sick general came about and settled into the run that would take it up the long reach of the river, around the bend, and out of sight from Ile aux Noix. The tall brigadier turned back toward the camp of the army which, by inheritance, he now commanded.

Fifteen years earlier, Montgomery had walked here in a red coat. Then he had had a captain's responsibility in his 17th of Foot, a good regiment of tightly controlled and disciplined soldiers, trained to instinctive obedience. Now, in 1775, there was still evidence of the old French works and of the camp that Captain Montgomery had seen in such disarray after the British bombardment and the hasty retreat of the French. The untidiness of the American camp through which General Montgomery now walked to his headquarters was the result of a devastation more damaging than the explosion of a 13-inch mortar bomb. Two retreats on Ile aux Noix within ten days had driven the list of the really sick to nearly the 50 per cent mark. Confidence in leadership had been lost in debate and argument which, not being confined within the bounds of rank, made every private a general. The Connecticut men showed their own shaken self-confidence in truculence toward

their two New York generals, one gone (and good rid-
dance) and one walking proud through the camp where
indolent but vociferous patriots lounged. Whereas the New
Englanders had been under arms for three months or more,
a fact which presupposed some training, the New Yorkers
had been in the army for a month or less, and that time had
been spent in the journey north. After their panic in the
night, the Yorkers had been left with the cohesion of a hand-
ful of sawdust, swept from a tavern floor. General Montgomery would have to have a strong arm and, with the
Connecticut men, keep a flexible wrist, if he was to use this
army against the enemy before him.

In spite of the two failures, Montgomery's plan still was
to encircle St. Jean. Once in position, even his poor grade
troops could contain and eventually could starve out the
five hundred trained regulars holed up in the fort. But until
the British soldiers on the Richelieu gave in, the way to
Montreal was denied the American general.

Hope come to the new commander of the Northern
Army's field force on the very day that he assumed the
responsibility for implementing the Congressional orders
to liberate Canada. Reinforcements arrived, having met
Schuyler's boat on their way. Standing at the landing place
with Lieutenant Colonel Seth Warner, Montgomery liked
the look of the new officers as Warner introduced each in
his turn. They doffed their hats politely in salute to their
general. Their hands were rough and work-hardened, as
Montgomery clasped each one in a firm welcoming hand-
shake. Colonel Warner's men were the new Green Mountain Boys, authorized by Congress to be raised out of Ethan

Allen's old band. They had not elected a colonel, neither wanting nor wishing to repudiate their old King Catamount, Ethan Allen. Lieutenant Colonel Warner led them. Since the days of the capture at Fort Ti, the wild boys of the Green Mountains had become serious about the grand cause of liberty. Old Merchant Curtenius of New York had procured green and red uniforms for the boys. Montgomery noticed how the soldiers filled the new green coats, and he noticed too the active way in which they secured their boats, slung their equipment, and followed their officers and sergeant off to their bivouac area.

Hard behind the one hundred and seventy Green Mountain Boys came Colonel Timothy Bedel's one hundred New Hampshire Rangers, woodsmen all. With Colonel Bedel came an independent company of volunteers. They were alert young men, many of whom were students at Dartmouth College. Fidelity and future leadership could be expected from this group.

On 17 September, Brigadier General Montgomery committed his army to the investing of St. Jean. He had begun the operation during the busy day of departure and arrival, the day he had assumed command. On that day, Major John Brown, with some one hundred and twenty men of his following, had been infiltrated to waylay convoys on the road from Montreal to St. Jean and that other British fort at Chambly. On that same day, Montgomery had organized his river flotilla of armed bateaux and gunboats. He gave command of that force to the unusually thin Commodore Douglas of Connecticut (who was dying of tuberculosis), charging him with the safety of the water-borne

flank of the army as it moved downriver and occupied the
old works that had been built on 6 September.

Major John Brown made his first catch of a British supply train on the night that Montgomery's army took up
its position south of St. Jean. Brown laid his ambush on
the Montreal road between the safe house of his first clandestine visit to Canada and the T-junction leading to St.
Jean and Chambly. When the work had been done, in the
bright moonlight to the accompaniment of sounds of shooting and shots that did little actual harm, the major counted
his gains. Twenty wagons were jack-knifed along the road.
At the head of each team a New Englander made soothing
noises to the restive, nervous horses. The oxen just stood
where they had been abandoned, their heads drooping under the heavy yoke-beams. Going from wagon to wagon,
Major Brown peered or felt into each one. Most of them
were loaded with artillery stores, the capture of which
denied the enemy rather than helped the Americans. The
four hogsheads, Brown knew from the rich heavy smell
and the size of the group gathered around them, were filled
with West Indian rum. He set a guard over the big barrels,
as he did over the wagons that he found filled with winter
clothing. A few drovers sat hunched against a fence, their
guard a bulky silhouette perched on the top rail like an
alert owl. Whatever escort there was for the convoy had
now slipped away; they would give an alarm at the fort.

At sun-up, the British came out of the fort at St. Jean.
They brought two light field guns which came rattling
into action when the scouts saw the roadblock and breastwork that Major Brown's men had thrown up. Covered by

the guns, the hundred British regulars charged. Firing as they went, Brown and his intruders fell back into the deep woods where the captured wagons were hidden.

In the American camp south of St. Jean, where Colonel Bedel was parading his five hundred men for the march around the British fort, they heard the firing. Brigadier General Richard Montgomery was called from his tent. For a full minute he stood beside Bedel, both men alert and listening. The distant thumping sound came again, the sound of musketry was sensed, felt, implied rather than heard. Montgomery lunged forward into a fast walk. Colonel Bedel was immediately behind him, pausing only long enough to shout to his troops the order to follow. As the sound of musketfire separated itself from the rustling of crisp leaves under hurrying feet, the American rangers spread out. The New Hampshire men and the Green Mountain Boys moved more cautiously, their muskets carried high in quick hands. Their trained eyes began to pick out from the gray trunks of forest trees the taut backs of Major Brown's men, who looked over and grinned as the fresh soldiers passed through. Some, in skirmish line, walked wide around where a little group tended a wounded officer. His naked torso, from which they had stripped the coat and shirt, was harshly white against the red and gold autumn leaves. The British were at the roadblock, being engaged by musketfire from the edge of the wood, when Montgomery came to a place from which he could see. The gun teams were coming up to take out the guns. As they dashed off at a gallop, the red-coated infantry left the breastworks and ran back toward St. Jean.

As the men of Brown's, Bedel's and Warner's commands
filtered out of the woods or returned from pursuit of the
fleeing "lobster backs," Montgomery talked with the officers. The place at the T-junction would be Colonel Bedel's
camp and strong point. The other two, Warner and Brown,
were to roam the back country as far as La Prairie and
Longeuil, on the right bank of the St. Lawrence opposite
Montreal. Ethan Allen was near the town of Sorel, where
the Richelieu enters the St. Lawrence. He had already
raised two hundred and fifty Canadians, and in a week's
time, he boasted, he would have two thousand at his back,
all loyal, true, and liberty-loving.

On returning to the south side of St. Jean, Brigadier
General Montgomery found the indifferent Connecticut
troops digging the siege-works. The ground into which the
rockhill Yankee farmers dug was shallow. Two feet down
in the mortar pits they found water. Their camp area was
not much better. When the cold rains came, as they did
toward the end of September, the camp area became a
morass. The men grumbled as they scrounged around for
material, *any* material, to raise their bedding up out of the
wet. For some reason the Connecticut soldiers blamed their
discomfort on the New Yorkers in command; their every
cough was a curse of York.

The pride of the mortar battery, which somehow was
dug, drained, and banked against steady British bombardment, was the 8-inch piece. It crouched in its bed like a
brass-green bullfrog on a mossy log. Much was expected
of it by the haphazard militiamen who came by to gawk
at this wonderful engine of war. But when the gunners

touched her off with a very satisfactory roar, the bomb-shell fell short of the enemy fort a mile and a quarter away. Laboriously, the artificers reamed out the powder pocket at the bottom of the 8-inch tube. The added powder capacity, however, was too much for the casting of the trunnions. After a very few shots a trunnion sheared off, leaving the handsome piece broken and useless, lying canted in its bed. It was remarked with cheerful resignation that no 8-inch mortar shells were left in the magazine. And after all, John Lamb, the master gunner, was a New York City man!

On 6 October the "Old Sow" arrived from Ticonderoga with boatloads of the big 13-inch shells. Working quickly, Montgomery's gunners had the big mortar set up by the following day. In the evening, the "Old Sow" lobbed seven great bombs toward the British fort. From a safe distance, Benjamin Trumbull, the Connecticut chaplain, pointed out to the group of home colony officers with whom he stood that the king's gunners returned twenty-four shots to Montgomery's seven.

Subject to sneers and criticism, the commanding general of the expeditionary force in Canada was a prisoner in his own siege camp south of the British fort. By the standards of his British Army days, the insubordination of the Connecticut troops was nothing short of intolerable mutiny. But a wider view had come to the captain of the 17th Foot since, as Richard Montgomery, he had become an active political Whig, had emigrated to the American colonies, and had assumed a leading military role in the Whig rebellion in his new homeland. He listened, now, to the popular voice of dissent and, though often questioning its wisdom, acceded to the clamor. On occasion, Brigadier General Montgomery even suffered a direct order to be disobeyed, his only solace being the hope that it was for the good of the service. When, in the normal course of the siege, Montgomery decided that the best approach for the storming party was against the southwest bastion, he determined to build a battery to breach the walls at that most vulnerable spot. Headquarters issued the necessary emphatic orders, and the clearing of brush at the inland end of the siege line began at once. Some of the Connecticut officers who were stationed on the American left doubted that the new battery would be either effective or practical. Others pointed out the great fatigue involved in hauling the guns to that place.

Colonel David Waterbury, second in rank to the general, forced a council of war at which he proposed that the new battery be placed at the opposite end of the American line, on the east bank of the Richelieu River. This battery, he argued, would be more defensive and effective against the terrible British vessel, the *Royal Savage*, still feared, still to come out. With the phalanx of Connecticut officers watching him stonily, and with the Connecticut troops hovering near at hand, Brigadier General Montgomery arose to give his decision. Though a council could advise and urge, the weighing of evidence and ultimate choice were the general's alone. Colonel Waterbury's, and Connecticut's, only alternative was to obey, or, as militiamen of a sovereign state, not mustered into the army of the Continental Congress, to withdraw from the expedition

and return to defend their homes at closer range. The temper of the troops was for the latter course. Quietly, Richard
Montgomery spoke. He gave his consent to the new battery
being built across the river, and, by submitting, kept the
army intact, if on an inactive defensive. The victorious
Connecticut troops considered themselves justified in their
strategy when a chance shot from their battery did, indeed,
sink the *Royal Savage*. But the army on the south side of
St. Jean was no nearer to capturing the British troops in
the fort than on the day in early September when the first
British shell reached out to them and they retired on Ile
aux Noix.

"To satisfy the troops," General Montgomery gave up
his plan to storm and assault the enemy fort. Next, the
plagued commander was asked to condone measures antic-
ipating a withdrawal.

It was Commodore Douglas, sometime captain of a mer-
chantman, who conceived the new strategy. As a few
friends sat down to dine with him in the comfort of his
cabin, with the rain beating down on the deck overhead,
the thin commodore weighed every alternative. Most vivid
was the possibility of an overwhelming British fleet forcing
him to give up his position on the right flank of the siege
line in order to save his fleet by falling back behind the
boom at Ile aux Noix. Douglas realized that in such an
event the west end of the American lines would be exposed
to enfilade fire from British boats in the river. In a carefully
prepared memorandum, Commodore Douglas proposed that
a riverbank battery be prepared on the west side of the
Richelieu River, presumably to work in conjunction with

the new battery on the east shore. Montgomery chose to ignore this suggestion. The Yankee skipper then turned to ingenuity. Going on shore, Douglas found a number of off-duty soldiers who, for "a handsome treat"—meaning a drunk on rum—would build the commodore his battery where he wanted it. This they did, and three "smart" guns were found to mount in the embrasures. Douglas's battery was Yankee trading at its nicest. The off-duty soldiers did not get their rum, not because the kindly skipper from Con-necticut would not give it to them, but because the Yorker quartermaster would not honor the commodore's requisi-tion. Beyond his refusal to issue the rum, Brigadier Gen-eral Montgomery took no notice of the battery, nor was any disciplinary action taken against his fleet commander.

Through all the autumn days of the general's humilia-tion the siege of St. Jean continued. Only by forbearance and his strict self-discipline was Montgomery able to keep the Connecticut men in the lines and at their tasks. He could not use them in the precise work of storming the enemy fortress, where the honed blade of trust must fit to courage as a bayonet does to a musket barrel. Nor could the guns, too small, too few, and poorly sighted for the job, effect the breach necessary to let in the storming troops. But General Montgomery maintained his siege line south of St. Jean, and from it the guns fired daily in a brave and noisy show of anger. From the British counterfire there were a few casualties, which the Connecticut men accepted, pence, shilling, and pound spent for Yankee freedom.

With his plan for an offensive turned into a blockade,

the general had to look elsewhere for victory. The view from his favorite observation point was good. Across the intervening ground he could see where the British Jack hung limply from its staff in the rain. Under its sodden folds, behind the earth and pickets of the walls, virtually all of the British regulars in Canada sheltered and waited. As long as they were there, the walls of Quebec were without defenders against the attack which, any day, Colonel Arnold's army would surely be making on that city. True, the defiant fort, whose flag was now whipping in a sudden wind squall, stood between him and that other Canadian city of the river, Montreal. There still remained a month of time. Looking beyond the tossing flag to the sky where dark storm clouds scudded, General Montgomery knew that time worked for him. Colonel Bedel held his post on the supply road north of St. Jean. No wagons with food and clothing and ammunition were going into the beleaguered garrison. John Brown had seen to that. An emissary had come from the Indians at Caughnawaga with overtures of peace and neutrality, perhaps even help. James Livingston and Moses Hazen, the latter having thought better of siding with the Crown, were raising regiments of Canadians among the French and English on the lower reaches of the Richelieu. Back at the general's headquarters, Jeremiah Duggan of Chambly was waiting to discuss a plan to run the river with cannon to invest the old stone fort at Chambly, twelve miles downstream from St. Jean. Eighty-eight British regulars were in the Chambly fort, all under command of an honorable but ineffectual gentleman named Joseph Stopford, major of the 7th Foot. Brigadier

General Montgomery walked back to his headquarters through the seemingly never-ending rain. Soon, now, the British soldiers in St. Jean would come to terms of surrender.

In the evening of 13 September, Duggan, now by courtesy a captain, loaded two good bateaux with a 9-pounder cannon and their stores. Covered by darkness, the boats shoved off from the new battery on the east shore of the river. They passed safely through Commodore Douglas's watch line. There were seventy Canadians in the bateaux, all experienced rivermen, including seven French cannoneers who had last served the guns with the revered Marquis de Montcalm. Gliding quickly down the rain-swollen river, the two boats scudded by the river-watch at St. Jean. Carefully now, with a lifetime's knowledge of the Richelieu setting every pole, the bateaumen let their craft down through the river rapids. It was about four o'clock in the morning when they heard through the darkness ahead the roar of the great cascade that drops the river down to the swirls and eddies licking at the walls of the fort below. Backing starboard and hauling port, Duggan's men turned the two bateaux into shore on the high ground above Chambly. James Livingston, Timothy Bedel, and John Brown, the ubiquitous uncle of Benedict Arnold and commander of the operation against Fort Chambly, were on the bank of the river to help Jeremiah Duggan ashore.

9

Height of Land, Height of Courage

In Captain Hanchet's company, Major Meigs's division, it was four men to each bateau for the last day's march over the Great Portage from the Kennebec to the Dead River. It was a four-mile carry. Abner Stocking and the other three Connecticut men had carried their bateau for the first mile, to the ridge above the last pond, where they had stopped to rest before taking their long, heavy burden down into the wide valley of the Dead River. They could glimpse the snaking coils of the stream in the distance. The boats of Greene's and Morgan's divisions were little black objects moving westward over the shining water. The high magnificence of a long great mountain followed the progress of the boats, its jagged summit cutting harshly into the blue sky. The rain of the preceding days had fallen as snow on the mountain's two peaks, and the upper flanks sparkled, too, with the first snow of autumn.

What Stocking and his companions looked at most carefully, as they sat on the gunwales of the bateau, was the wide savannah that stretched for two miles from the foot of the ridge to the river. The flat land looked like an ideal place over which to carry a heavy bateau—if one *had* to carry a bateau. But the men of the division, returning for a second load, had told them that the quiet savannah was a terrible place, a morass, a bog, a swamp of clinging brush and sucking calf-deep mud. Even Colonel Arnold in his high boots, the men said, would get his feet wet crossing that place. While Stocking and the others prolonged their rest, the two oxen that Major Meigs so greatly cherished breasted the rise and shambled on down the road. Their two soldier-drovers, unencumbered by burdens other than their goads, ambled behind their charges. Though the beasts were thin, as thin and lean as the men of the division, to the four men on the bateau they looked like rich, luscious meat, bits sizzling at the end of a green birch twig, lumps bubbling up in a pot, with dumplings to absorb the fat. Stocking had heard of someone who had eaten a partridge two days before; someone else had talked with a rifleman who said that the scouts had seen a moose and many signs up ahead, where the army was headed. On the Dead River there would be fresh moose meat for all. There even was hopeful talk that the barrels of foul-tasting salt pork would be left to rot in the woods. A soldier of Greene's division, who paused by the men on the boat, told them to save the pork for bait, because in the placid waters of the Dead River there were fine trout for a soldier's supper. Then Captain Goodrich came up, with his big black dog following at his heels, and ordered Stocking and his men to get on.

They crossed the terrible savannah, sometimes with the

carrying poles on their shoulders, where a stumble by the man at the other end bruised the surface bones even through the padding they had contrived. They tried carrying the bateau at waist-level, but the drag burned their arm muscles, and too often aching hands lost their grip. In a few places they could drag and push the boat along. At last, at three o'clock in the afternoon, they came to a rivulet where they could launch the bateau. Stocking and the others had time to load the boat with stores and row a mile up the river before making camp for the night.

In the next four days Stocking, with the other bateaux of Hanchet's company, traveled forty-seven miles up the winding course of the Dead River. Colonel Arnold, in his dugout canoe, overtook Abner Stocking on 16 October, the day after the hard carry over the savannah. The colonel waved and called out a greeting as he shot past them. The men in the bateau shouted back, and pulled just a bit harder on their oars.

For two long hours the Indian paddlers pulled the canoe through the quiet water. So crooked was the course of the river that the colonel felt as though he were going nowhere at all. Always, it seemed, the big mountain filled the view, its top dipped in snow like a sugar confection. First on the left, then on the right, and again over the bobbing back of the Indian, paddling in the bow.

After the river straightened out, Arnold passed Morgan's division of riflemen, stretched out in idleness for a quarter of a mile along the grassy bank. The soldiers appeared to be preoccupied with doing nothing. Daniel Morgan, big and solid, came down to the water's edge. He was in breechcloth and Indian leggings, showing an expanse of naked thigh and buttocks. He cried out to Arnold that he had let Greene's division go through. The riflers, he assured Arnold, were in fine shape and would take over the lead of the army again after a little rest and a meal.

At last Colonel Arnold left the big mountain behind him, with the course of the river leading into the northwest. He passed by Natanis's cabin, high on a flat bluff with cleared land all around it, and a pleasant prospect. Three miles beyond the incongruous house alone in the wilderness, Arnold found Lieutenant Colonel Greene's division and went ashore, tired and stiff from his long hours in the canoe.

In the morning, a fine one overhead, Greene showed Arnold the two barrels of flour left to his division. The other barrels had been sprung in the carries and wetted in the swamps and the rain, and in the sloshing water in the leaky bateaux. The salt pork had fared better; Greene had ten barrels of it.

The camp site was a good one, and the two senior officers of the expedition decided to halt there, while a detail went back to draw reserve stores from Enos's division. The men of Greene's division would rest, catch fish, perhaps hunt, and, to make use of the time, roll cartridges with the paper and bulk powder that they had. Meigs's and Morgan's men would do the same when they came up.

At noon the rifle companies arrived, on their way through to take up the lead which they had briefly relinquished. They came as Major Bigelow was setting out with the ration party. For a time all was confusion, as the boats going up mingled in the narrow water with the boats going down. At last, to the bawling orders of Daniel Morgan, the riflemen's boats pulled in to shore. The confusion then transferred itself to the shore, as the Pennsylvanians and Virginians moved through the camp, mingling boisterously with their New England comrades in arms. When the fraternization was over, Greene's division had even less food than before the riflemen came through. Around the first bend upriver, the riflemen pulled from under their loose shirts the loot they had found in the musketmen's camp.

The rain, which begun to fall on Thursday, 19 October, continued without letup all day Friday and through Saturday. It fell hard and fast, driven by gusty winds that danced around the points of the compass like contrary demons. It drenched the army that was spread out all along the Dead River from the Great Carry to the narrow valley approaching the first of the chain of ponds. Those who pressed on with the boats were as wet and miserable as those plodding the shoreline. Some of the men made shelters and sat dejectedly in the dripping rain.

Dr. Senter made the best of it. On Friday night the doctor and his medical team ate their last good meal. On that day Colonel Enos had killed his ox; Meigs's oxen had been butchered two days earlier. Senter and each of his team had drawn a pound of beef. At the day's end they pitched their tent and made their stew. Dr. Senter added the last of his potatoes and carrots, brought all the way from Fort Weston. To make a night of it, the doctor rummaged in his medicine chest and brought out his butter box.

This delicacy fried the trout the men had caught and soaked into the dumplings. So they feasted in the rain. That night they slept, replete.

Benedict Arnold left Colonel Greene's camp on Saturday, 21 October. It was still raining, and he noted that the river had risen and the current was more swift. The headquarters group went a mile beyond where Morgan's division was encamped and went ashore for the night. What with making camp, drying their clothes and preparing the half-rations which were their fare, they did not doss down until nearly eleven o'clock. At four o'clock in the morning Arnold wakened out of a deep sleep. Everywhere about him in the dark was the sound of an ominous force. It was the sound that a flock of mallards makes, coming in low overhead to the decoys. But the sound is frozen at the first startling moment that the hunter hears it. As Arnold woke more fully, he became aware of a gentle lapping of water close to where his blankets cocooned his feet. Wide awake now, the colonel was on his feet, shouting that the river was in flood. For the next few minutes the headquarters group splashed around in the wet darkness, groping for their baggage and carrying it to higher ground behind the bivouac.

Arnold and his staff spent the last hours of the night huddled in miserable conjecture as to the damage taking place at all the other camps on the Dead River gone wild. At dawn they saw the land flooded. The quiet river had disappeared into a wild lake, with bays and islands, and with trees growing incongruously out of the shallow water. Somewhere in that expanse lay the river channel, lost to the bateaux. The soldiers of the army who marched along the riverbank were forced far back to the water's edge and scattered. Already the army had lost three days' travel and had eaten up three days' rations because of the rain. The flood would cost it more food, more wasted days. In the stillness after the storm, with the flood water lying tranquilly on the land, the army and its commander were face to face with disaster or decision. Colonel Arnold chose decision. He sent his aides out to summon all the officers they could find for a council of war.

They came in three groups: the rifle officers with Morgan from the front of the army; Major Meigs and those of his officers in the river party by bateau, gaily, as if coming to a husking bee; the land party came down the big brook that flowed into the Dead River from the west. They were a little bit sheepish for having taken a wrong turning. They had strayed, been lost, and finally had found their way. All the officers showed the stain and strain of the march, yet even those who were sick tried to conceal the tremors that shook them as they bowed in salute to Colonel Arnold, seated, his leg cocked, on a flat-topped boulder.

In the orderly course of a council of war, the most junior officer speaks first. Arnold listened to the subalterns, each in turn, then to the seven captains who were present, and finally, to Major Meigs. Giving close attention, he heard the accounts of accidents, sickness, and ever the scarcity of food. From the officers who lived, worked, slept, and ate with the men, he heard of and judged the morale of the troops. Though they talked of the trials of the Kennebec, the Great Portage, the Dead River, and the flood-lake, their gestures of emphasis and the glance of their eyes were all upstream, in the direction of the Height of Land, the Chaudière, and Quebec.

The final word in a council of war lies with the commander. Alone, now, on the rock of his confidence, Benedict Arnold told, rather than proclaimed, his decision. In announcing his orders, Arnold accepted compliance with casualness. He was going to Quebec; the others could follow him. That they would follow him was a simple, natural conclusion.

Rising, now, and standing upon the rock, better to see the individual officers to whom he was to speak, Colonel Arnold detailed the new method of advance into Canada. He first picked out Oliver Hanchet. Chaudière Pond, he told the captain, was approximately twenty-seven miles away. Hanchet would go there at once with fifty men to handle provisions that would be coming from the French settlements below. Arnold himself (he had raised his voice and his eyes to include the whole group of officers) would go on ahead of Captain Hanchet to buy the food. At the same time and place he would get news from inside Quebec City, and word of the progress of General Schuyler's army. The army would come on, but (Arnold's eyes flicked quickly to where a young lieutenant, flushed with fever, sat fighting the will of heavy eyelids to close) the sick and the weakest of the men would be sent back to Fort Weston. Only the number of men would go on to Canada whom the army could supply with provisions for fifteen days. Before that fortnight was out they would be eating French beef and "sass" from the good gardens of the habitants. On that high note the council ended, the captains going off to make their lists and count their stores.

On the day that Colonel Arnold reduced the size and the fighting strength of the army, seven of the bateaux overset in the rapids of the swollen river. All the food they carried was lost. The expedition continued its march into the narrowing valley leading to the Height of Land. That night two inches of snow fell.

Twenty-six men of Meigs's and Morgan's divisions were sent back. The sick officer who went with them carried the orders to Colonel Greene and Colonel Enos to trim down their commands according to the new formula: fifteen days' rations to every man going forward. In Greene's division the food situation was desperate. Major Bigelow, who had gone back to draw flour from the army stores, returned with but two barrels, or two pounds of flour per man. But Christopher Greene and his three captains were staunch in their resolve, trusting in the Almighty to provide, and in Benedict Arnold to lead them. The men of the companies were dispirited but not downhearted. They would follow their officers anywhere to find food. The best chance of getting the meals they talked about, and the meals that followed them into their dreams, was at the French settlements. Colonel Arnold had gone there to fetch them back their banquet. The hungry men of Greene's division helped forty-eight of their sickest and weakest men into three bateaux, to go back to the coast. From the spilled-over banks of the Dead River, standing in the new snow, they watched their friends away on the horrible road that had cost them all but hope.

In Colonel Enos's 4th Division, only seven men were eligible to return to the Maine settlements. The three companies of the division had always been in the rear of the army. Like the others, they had struggled with the river. But when they came to the portages the way was clear, the roads improved by the others who had gone before them. Their weariness came from the multiple carries they had had to make to bring forward the extra stores. They had come to identify the food they lugged as their own, to be jealously guarded from the strangers ahead, whom they had not seen on all the long journey. Few, if any, of Enos's men had seen Colonel Arnold since the early stages of the march. Arnold had spent the night of 9 October with Captain Samuel McCobb and his men. Since that night, over two weeks before, Benedict Arnold's leadership had been a distant thing, growing rusted with the interminable days of labor, like a hatchet left untended in the grass.

On receiving and digesting Arnold's orders to advance, Colonel Enos hurried forward with five of his officers to attend a consultation with Colonel Greene. Colonel Enos took the chair. Lieutenant Peters, who was of the 4th Division, immediately proposed that both Enos's and Greene's divisions turn back. One by one, the grim-faced officers rose to speak, making every telling point for survival. When the motion was put to a vote, Colonel Greene, Major Bigelow, and the three company commanders were

firm for following Arnold. The vote was a tie. For a
moment, Colonel Enos vacillated, then finally opted for
return with his officers and men.

In the wrangling that followed, Enos's company commanders flatly refused to give stores to officers and men
so mad as to think that they could go on. At first, Colonel
Enos's intercessions were brushed aside by Captains Williams, McCobb, and Scott, over whom he had lost all personal and military control. Eventually they allowed the
colonel to release two and a half barrels of flour. Forced to
be content with this pittance, Colonel Greene sent his own
men to take the barrels away. Nothing remained between
the two groups of officers but a gulf of silent contempt
and a wall of faithless rationalization. The thirty-eight-year-
old colonel from Rhode Island left the conference restored
and encouraged by his own pride and honor. The forty-
six-year-old colonel from Connecticut watched the other
man go before he himself turned back. The officers of the
4th Division expressed regret at seeing such a brave man
go foolishly to his doom.

The news of Enos's disaffection traveled slowly from
the rear of the army to the front. Weak men, carrying one
of the few remaining bateaux over a short portage on the
upper Dead River, heard of it from the tired men who
gave them a hand as they came by. They put the bateau
down to curse the cowards. On the chain of ponds that
made up the final steps to the Height of Land, hungry men
stopped in utter disbelief when the news was shouted to
them by the stumbling marchers along the shore. The
riflemen, guarding the precious remnants of their com-

pany's food piled in the grass on the high meadow that looked down on Chaudière Pond and the wide plain of Canada, spat disdainfully in contempt of New England. Colonel Arnold did not learn of Enos's defection then. He was driving down the Chaudière River, drawing near to the first Canadian habitation.

The line of march from the Height of Land to Chaudière Pond was well "advertised" by Colonel Arnold himself. The compass course, he wrote in an open letter to the officers, was north by east; the distance approximately six miles. In the advertisement, Arnold warned against following the brook, which would only lead them into the swamp from which it was impossible to escape. Arnold sent the message by Isaac Hull to the rendezvous of the army at the beautiful meadow. Hull it was who would show them the beginning of the portage and conduct them safely from the swamp.

Colonel Greene, too, had received a letter from Colonel Arnold, a letter addressed also to Colonel Enos. In it, Arnold urged that the bateaux be left behind and the army proceed on foot, each man carrying what he could. Arnold pointed out that there already were four bateaux (those of Captain Hanchet) on Chaudière Lake, and that the transporting of the clumsy craft had been brutal work. However, Greene would have to bring bateaux to carry any sick that he might have.

With the commander's instruction and advice, Lieutenant Colonel Greene organized the movement of the expedition down from the Height of Land. Daniel Morgan, whose

men, he vowed, were still up to the task, elected to take
seven bateaux with him to the Chaudière. In the bateaux
would be military stores that would be needed in the attack
on Quebec City. Captain Henry Dearborn, having found
as if by chance an Indian birch canoe and paddles, decided
to take it along. For the rest, they left the patched and
worn craft where they had set them down. It was also
decided that each man would make his own way to the
Chaudière and down the river until he met the food that
Arnold had promised. The flour and the remaining scraps
of salt pork were distributed in equal shares. Each mess immediately built a fire to make ash cakes, which the Pennsylvanians called "bleary." Dr. Senter, who distributed the tiny
gray cakes, five to each of the medical detachment, called
them fit for a Lilliputian, and named the concoction "Lil-
lipu." As each group completed its preparations, the men
hunched their packs, took up their muskets, and followed
after the party that had gone before, guided and piloted
by Isaac Hull.

To walk along a side hill and keep one's elevation is difficult at best. When one is tired and weak, to keep the higher
ground is impossible. One by one, the slowly marching
parties came down off the Height of Land. The direction
set by Arnold was lost in confusion of blow-downs and
spruce thickets. Isaac Hull himself was as lost as the pur-
blind drummer whom Volunteer Henry led by hand and
voice through the forest tangle.

If Schaeffer, the drummer, was a pathetic figure, his
clothes torn to rags, his bleary cakes stolen, yet with his

drum on his shoulder, there was nothing pathetic about Mrs. Sergeant Greer. The seventen-year-old John Joseph Henry was walking just behind her when the neck of land on which they were marching petered out into a swamp, three-quarters of a mile wide. Snow was on the tussocks, and windowpane ice covered the water between. Without hesitation, Mrs. Greer hiked her skirts up to her waist and stepped off into the knee-deep, icy water. The boy Henry followed the large white legs of the sergeant's wife as they churned and broke the ice-scabs all the way across the wasteland. At one of the halts on a mound in another bog, they lost a second woman, who, too, had marched with her husband all the way from Lancaster, in Pennsylvania. Private Warner, who had been perhaps the weakest of Smith's riflemen, was missing at one of the rest stops. Mrs. Warner, who had not yet sat down to rest, went alone down the back track, looking for her husband. The soldiers waited an hour. Then, pressed by the urgency to get out of the swamp before dark, they moved on.

Mrs. Warner found her husband lying where he had fallen, on the dry edge of the swamp. She could not lift him, nor could he help himself. Private Warner died during the night. In the morning, his wife covered him decently with frosty leaves. Then she took up his rifle and, with it cradled in her arms, set out after her company. For twenty miles she marched alone. Then, catching up with a detachment of Meigs's division, the young widow was taken in by them.

The swamps, the windfalls, and the dense spruce and alder thickets that entrapped Arnold's men lay to the

south of Chaudière Pond and all around the irregularly
shaped pond that lay just to the east. The soldiers, who in
their weariness had been drawn down from the higher
ground, stuck doggedly to the shoreline of the east pond.
Surely over the next wooded point the walking would be
better. But it seemed that every new view of meandering
shoreline showed only another deep bay, with yet another
marsh at its tip. Through all these marshes ran a water
course through which the men must march, knee deep,
waist deep, shoulder deep. Near the mouth of one of these
streams that had the depth and width of a small river, Captain Dearborn found his friend William Goodrich.

Night was coming on, and Captain Goodrich was "near
beat out." For hours, he had been plumbing the river at
armpit depth, searching for a ford in the frigid and icy
water. His men, now joined by part of Dearborn's soldiers,
sat, half wet, half dry, on scattered bits of snow-covered
ground. Quaking with long, spasmodic shivers, the durable
captain from the Berkshire hills climbed into Dearborn's
bark canoe. Far down the pond the light of a fire winked
as it beckoned. The two captains hoped that it would be
the night camp of a bateau party. They wanted the boat
to ferry the men over the river. But at the beacon fire they
found only a single soldier, left behind by Captain Hanchet's advance ration party. During the night Captain
Goodrich dried out and warmed up, and in the morning
the two officers returned to their men, not having found a
bateau, but ready at once to start ferrying with the light
birchbark canoe. All morning the small craft carried the
men, one at a time, across the narrow river. In the after-

noon the whole long process was repeated at another river, only fifty rods beyond the first. That night the two captains again slept at the fire with their men around them.

Dearborn and Goodrich had been lucky. They had crossed the outlet of the east pond. Their men had been spared the tortuous march around the horrible shore; they had also been spared a whole day of torment such as the other companies would have to endure before meeting the food that was coming up the Chaudière River.

The seven bateaux belonging to the riflemen had already taken to the river when Captains Goodrich and Dearborn and their men started down. They soon caught up with the bateaux. The seven, and three more, all lay jumbled in the rapids below a waterfall. All were smashed, sunk, tipped over, shattered fragments jettisoned on the shore. Among all the dereliction of disaster was but one man, his drowned body wedged haphazardly between two rocks around which the rapids swirled. The last sentry was George Innes of Virginia.

It was on the way down the Chaudière that the dogs were eaten. Captain Dearborn's big black dog fed the men of Goodrich's company on the last day of October. The captain was too sick to eat at all. After the dogs, the men cooked their shot pouches, arguing feebly as to whether it was better to roast them or to boil them. Most of the men had not eaten for two days, and it was a test of Captain Goodrich's command that he left two quarters of dog for those coming on behind.

On Thursday, 3 November, when only fourteen miles

Captain Daniel Morgan

Captain Eleazar Oswald

Captain John Lamb

Lieutenant John André

A view of the city of Montreal.

Colonel Benedict Arnold

*N.Y. Public Library-
Print Collection*

American Rifleman

Portage on the Kennebec River at Norridgewock Falls.

Brigadier General
Richard Montgomery

*N.Y. Public Library-
Print Collection*

British Grenadier

*Brown University Library;
Mrs. John Nicholas Brown Collection*

A view of the city of Quebec.

from the first French settlement, Caleb Haskell of Ward's company heard the bleating of a calf. The others had heard it, too, and all stood motionless, listening and watching, as a little herd came ambling toward them from around a tag alder thicket. Small grinning Frenchmen in warm coats and toque hats were driving the beasts, and they made it clear that one of these was for butchering, there and then. The habitants left the calf with the fife player, Caleb Haskell, and the army coming down the Chaudière River found food at last.

There was more food, beef, butter, fowl, eggs, fresh bread, and vegetables, and there was some rum and brandy too in Sartigan. There was warm clothing for the most needy, and beds with husk mattresses where the Americans slept, jumbled among the Frenchmen who smelled of onions and stale tobacco, and who were very kind. As their strength returned, and since for the most part they were young it returned quickly, the individuals pulled themselves into an army again. The news from Quebec was good. The British in the city were few, the habitants well disposed toward the American liberators, and it was rumored that General Schuyler had won a great victory over the regulars. That the approach of Arnold's army was known in Quebec no longer matter. Surprise had been achieved, though the numbers, route, and intent had been told to the governor by the trusted Indians, Sabatis and Eneas. In spite of their treachery, British troops had been free to go to the defense of Quebec, and there had been time for fear to weaken the courage of the townspeople.

So the men of Arnold's army, who for thirty-one days had
been alone against the wilderness and the weather, who
had overcome every privation and had come over the
Height of Land, were contemptuously insolent when their
talk turned to the last obstacle, the fortified walls of Quebec
City.

Major Meigs left Sartigan for St. Mary's on Sunday,
5 November. Colonel Arnold had given him much to do
before the army came marching down the river. He had to
buy stores and supplies of every kind, and he had to find
and purchase bark canoes to ferry the soldiers across the
wide St. Lawrence. No commander could count on the
British leaving any boats on the south shore.

There was a time during the army's progress from Sartigan to the St. Lawrence when the men wryly recalled
the Kennebec and the Dead River and the Great Carry
between. Below St. Mary's the way to Point Levis, across
from Quebec City, left the Chaudière River for the Etchemin. In a long march through new snow, the canoe detachment portaged thirty big bark canoes. Again, four men
hoisted their craft onto their shoulders and marched away
under leaden skies. But the canoes were light, compared
to the heavy bateaux of former carries, and there were no
barrels of flour and pork, no powder, lead, or cartridges
to be lugged. The American soldiers were marching light
of foot and high of spirit. They were living off the land,
which was a friendly place, in spite of rising prices for
their wants and needs. Coming a day or two behind the
now small companies were the invalids, the men lost,

strayed, exhausted in the swamp around the Chaudière Ponds. Their friends had given them up for dead. The Indians, that no one knew to be there, had found them, nursed them, and brought them safely in to Sartigan. When Natanis, who had been hunted on the Dead River, was found with a group of Abenakis, he was asked why he had not come forward before. He replied to Lieutenant Steele, "You would have killed me." Natanis now marched with the leading file of riflemen, and because of the friends he had returned, he was the friend of all.

The companies made the last day's march together, to the cadence of the drum and fife. The men scarcely slackened their pace for the last climb up to the high palisade that looked across to Quebec City. Those coming on behind saw their first enemy, a wet youth of fifteen, in the threadbare but elegant blue coat of a midshipman of the Royal Navy. The riflemen had caught him at the river's edge. Actually, they had fished him out of the water when he tried to swim to safety. To the American men who had dared the long, long march, he looked small, skinny, and bedraggled, this living symbol of England's naval might.

So, at last, Colonel Arnold's army came through to the St. Lawrence River and looked over to the city climbing up the rocks, crowned with spires and great roofs of green copper, roofs bigger by far than that of the biggest New England barn. Highest of all in the city of the river was the citadel on Cape Diamond, that seemed to anchor the city wall to the cliff. Upriver, a mile or so above the stern fort, a fissure, marked by trees and brush now leafless, cut through the steep escarpment. It showed the path up which James Wolfe had marched his army on the day, sixteen years before, when he had conquered the proud city of Quebec.

10

The Garrison of the Besieged

Among the officers of the 7th Foot who left Quebec City in June of 1775 to defend the Champlain Pass against the American rebels was an exquisite lieutenant on his first campaign. He wrote passionate poetry to an unattainable loved one in whom he had lost all interest except as the Ideal of Love. He illustrated his perceptive and witty diaries with adroit sketches. He played the flute and employed his knowledge of music in devising imaginative theatricals. That he had bought a commission in the fusileers was due to the fact that he wished to avoid the vulgarity of entering into the very successful family business, "in Trade." For two years he had avoided military duty by studying, in Germany, subjects remotely having to do with martial matters. Eventually called to follow his regiment to Canada, he chose to go there by way of Baltimore, Philadelphia, and Boston. Surprised by the vehemence of the fomenting rebellion, he hurried overland to Montreal and Quebec, making sketches as he went. To the war that in 1775 began as a rebellion of uncouth colonials, John

André brought a talent for quiet daring and a calm courage, inspiring alike to poets and to soldiers. To Major André, the war brought only the rebounding fame of failure.

The social life of Quebec City during the winter of 1774-75 was a new realm for exploration for André. The new lieutenant, who spoke fluent French, and German and Italian, was taken up by the society of the city. Before the winter was over he was forced to make a selection, from among his many invitations, of the houses where he would dine. There were picnics in the snow, to which the officers of the garrison rode out in sleighs. A favorite place for sliding was the ice cone in the St. Lawrence, below the high falls of Montmorency. In the moonlight or under the stars, it was a gay race or a quiet trot over the river ice to town, with a charming *Quebeçoise* sharing the fur lap robe. John André remarked the difference between the "silken dalliance" at Government House and the winter-training exercises in the crude fashion of the Indians, where he slept with his troops on fir branches in a covered pit dug into five feet of snow. After a day's hunting with a merciless Indian tutor, a spitted rabbit toasted over a fire of twigs tasted better than Smithfield ham served by the butler at the duke's sideboard. John André did not particularly like the life "à la Indian," but under General Guy Carleton he learned Indian ways and the way of soldiering in North America.

The idyll and agony of garrison life in the capital of Canada ended with the arrival of orders from Boston. Although Guy Carleton was governor and general in all Canada, the movement and disposal of troops in North

America were within the purview of General Thomas Gage. A dispatch boat, coming round from Boston, brought orders to Carleton to concentrate his forces on Lake Champlain. The order was published on 19 May. The following day, Moses Hazen, breathless with the bad news, arrived to tell of the fall of Ticonderoga and Arnold's capture of the sloop at St. Jean. For the 7th Foot, the urgency for an immediate departure increased. Another day brought another messenger. Ethan Allan had seized St. Jean for a second time in the same day, but the arrival of M. Belestre with the Montreal militia had driven the invader away. On 23 May, farewells said, the fusileers of the 7th Foot sailed away up the St. Lawrence.

Guy Carleton was bound for Montreal to set up headquarters and government in that city. The 7th went to the Richelieu River to garrison the forts above and below the rapids. At Chambly, Major the Honorable Joseph Stopford marched in under the old French coat of arms chiseled into the stone of the covered way. He stood, goldheaded stick in hand, as his officers marched into the Place d'Armes and dismissed their troops into the stone barracks. Stopford, the son of an Irish earl, was occupied in his own quarters when thirty women, with almost twice their number of children, trooped in and began the squabble over quarters. Stopford had ten officers and seventy-eight fusileers under command in the sturdy square fort with the four squat towers. Six tons of gunpowder, many muskets, cartridges, hand grenades, and a big supply of provisions were under the major's care in the old but sturdy citadel.

Lamenting his *canadienne* loves, yet with his fair Honora's miniature pinned over his yearning heart, Lieutenant André marched to the fort at St. Jean. But no fort was there, only the old brick barracks building and, a hundred yards away, another brick house with an adjacent wooden barn. When the troops from Quebec City arrived, the 26th Foot had already begun to rebuild the St. Jean fort. The fusileers joined in the work.

Along the lines and between the stakes set out by the engineers, carefully turfed earthen walls rose around the two brick buildings. A covered way was built, connecting the two redoubts, each of which encompassed a square of one hundred feet. A stockade went around three sides of the whole. Beyond, a good ditch was dug, its face set with a bristle of sharpened sticks. The fourth side of Fort St. Jean was the Richelieu River, at this point a quarter of a mile wide.

At the water's edge, an officer of the Royal Navy and a detachment from their vessel in the St. Lawrence were building a schooner. They called her *Royal Savage,* and her captain, Algee of the Senior Service, vowed to red-coated officers watching the planking cover the ribs that he would have the rebel navy in tow before the leaves fell to the ground.

The 14-gun *Savage* was launched and brought around to the fitters' dock during the early part of September. But by then the Yankees had landed, and held the mouth of the Richelieu River. Confined to a mile-long stretch of the quarter-mile wide river, Algee's big schooner became a fourth wall to Fort St. Jean.

If the navy was not ready to go out and give battle before the rebels came, the army was ready to receive them when they arrived. Major Charles Preston had a strong post, well built, well armed, and well stocked for a siege. Under the major's command were five hundred of the best and fittest soldiers in Canada, men of the 7th and Preston's own 26th Foot. He had forty trained gunners of the Royal Artillery, who, with helpers from the infantry, would serve forty-two cannon emplaced on the walls and at embrasures in the palisades. There were also seven iron mortars, with pits already dug. Monsieur Belestre was at St. Jean with his company of ninety loyal Frenchmen, who were useful as rangers and scouts and were infinitely more reliable than the bedecked savages who were camped a little apart.

On the day the rebels approached St. Jean, the Canadians and the Indians went out to harry them. From the high point of the southern redoubt, the watching group of British officers saw the string of men, Indians and Frenchmen indistinguishable from their dress, disappear into the woods west of the fort. A mile or so to the south, the Yankee boats were turning in to land. Major Preston passed his telescope to the artillery officer, who looked long at the little figures of men deploying in the big circle of the lens. He considered the range a possible one for the longer, heavier guns of his battery. With the major's permission, the gunner began the play of ranging on the distant enemy. The round shot was falling close. Through his glass the major could see the little figures scatter as the round shot fell nearby. A faint sound of musketry from the land side told the officers on the walls of the redoubt that M. Belestre had made contact and was worrying the Americans' flank.

When darkness came that night of 6 September, the rebels were still on the riverbank, though they had moved back out of range of the annoying British guns. The Indians were back, boasting and dancing a victory dance in their camp. Monsieur Belestre came in to dine, all smiles and quite willing to answer questions about his successful skirmish with the American "Pumpkins."

The British officers were on the ramparts early in the morning, eager to see what the rebels had done with the hours of darkness. Fieldworks had been begun, but work had ceased. Later in the morning activity increased in the enemy camp, but it was a movement to the boats, and when all were embarked and the English soldiers stood ready for an attack from the river, the Americans rowed away upstream. No one watching from Fort St. Jean believed that the Yankees had gone far, or that they would stay away for long. The siege of St. Jean had begun.

Major Preston's duty was to stay where he was, in the encompassing walls of his fort. While he was there, across the supply line between the base at Ticonderoga and the objective at Montreal, the Americans could not go past him. They would have to root the British out of St. Jean, and they would have to do this before winter set in and closed their vital link with faraway Ticonderoga. For Major Preston and his six hundred British and Canadians, there was no possibility of driving away the Americans. The only hope of a British victory lay with the arrival of reinforcements from England, or the coming of the winter ice, after which there would be no fresh regiment from home until the spring, and that was eight months away. In

two months' time the ice would be forming in the marshy
bays, the leaves would be gone, and snow would be driving
under the tent-flaps of the Yankees. The British troops settled down to the daily routine of confinement in their fort
for eight to ten weeks.

On 17 September, the Americans were back to stay. The
English officers of the 7th and the 26th now knew that
Brigadier General Richard Montgomery was in command
opposite them. Some of them remembered him as a captain
of the old 17th.

The following day Major Preston sent a detachment out
north of the fort to try to recapture a wagon train from
Montreal that had been waylaid by rebel bandits. The detachment encountered considerable resistance, and Preston
sent a second force to bring back the first. Both parties returned safely, with the intelligence that the rebels were
north of the fort in sizable numbers, that the road to Montreal was closed, and that St. Jean was invested. Lieutenant
André, who had gone out with the relief, saw his first battle casualty that day: the soldier seemed to lie almost com-
fortably in a meadow out in front of the little British field
gun that had killed him by mistake.

For the next month the British lived in boredom, discomfort, and dirt in their compound within the palisades. At the
first appearance of the enemy, Major Preston had brought
the women and children of the garrison into the safety of
the fort. There were between seventy and eighty of them
(the squirming scurrying of the children made an exact
count impossible). The ground outside the redoubts was
stamped into a mire by the cattle in their pens. In the space

between the two buildings and the earthen walls of the strong points, the tramping of all the feet churned the ground into rain-fed mud. Here most of the soldiers slept or spent the long nights in restlessness.

In the two brick houses which the Yankees in their tents and bivouacs so envied, the staff and the women and children lived in the close stench of overcrowded bodies.

Until 10 October, the enemy had been ineffectual and inactive. On that day the Yankees were seen dragging cannon and building a redoubt on the east bank of the river. The soldiers of the 7th and the 26th were turned out to build a traverse wall facing the new threat. Rain had made the ground soft as gruel, and more rain washed away the traverse wall. The arrival of the big mortar, the "Old Sow," added the chance of death to the misery of discomfort. A 13-inch shell crashed through the roof of the south barracks and exploded in a searing flash that shattered the windows and wrecked the rooms. A lieutenant and a soldier were killed, and five men were wounded. The number of graves in the little cemetery by the covered way increased the next day, and on the days that followed.

The schooner was sunk while there were still leaves on the trees. The boastful navy captain had gone on down to Chambly. When men with packs were seen hurrying northward on the east side of the river, the watching British officers guessed that they were going on to attack that other fort. No one in St. Jean saw the Yankee boats that slipped by in the dark of night, carrying cannon to bombard Fort Chambly.

The cattle pens were soon empty. Rations were cut to

two-thirds of the normal allowance. Eight cows, calmly munching the poor grass in the clearing between the ditch and the woods, brought the garrison to the walls to see such a wonderful, unattainable sight. When Capitaine Monin and Monsieur Moiquin strolled out and drove the little herd into the fort, the men were loudly cheered.

Eight thin cows did not provide a banquet for six hundred hungry people. Almost nightly, however, the garrison of the besieged diminished by a trickle. On the nights that Major Preston did not send a messenger to General Carleton for help, one or two Canadians slipped over the wall. But few militiamen were left by the time the icy rains of October had stripped the last brown leaves from the trees. The Indians had long since gone. Sometimes a messenger from Montreal was heard calling softly at the gate. Occasionally an American deserter came in the night and was let in at the point of a bayonet.

Through the summer months, while the soldiers on the Richelieu built their fort of earth and logs, Governor Carleton, in Montreal, strove to fashion an army out of the human fabric of his colony. Guy Carleton worked in a material as flaccid as cheesecloth. Only victory and success gave substance to his efforts, a substance which collapsed again at the first word of a defeat or a failure.

The rebellion had started badly for the governor general of a Canada alien to Britain in culture, religion, and language. The distant skirmishes of Lexington and Concord had been defeats for the army. To the habitant, the quick fall of the great stone fortress at Ticonderoga (which the French called "Carillon") was an even more vivid defeat.

Fifteen years before, the fall of Carillon to the strength of a British army had been the prelude to the defeat and subjugation of New France. When the dark-skinned *Bostonais*, Benedict Arnold, had taken the English sloop from St. Jean and the familiar figure of Ethan Allen had occupied the town, only the French Canadian Belestre had come in time to drive the *Bostonais* away. In the summer of 1775 there was small encouragement for the habitant to join Carleton's militia in defense of British Canada. Nor were the Indian auxiliaries, still largely influenced by French leaders, anxious to commit themselves to a side the soldiers of which appeared to be so easily humbled.

The arrival at the Richelieu forts and the sight of all the red-coated soldiers building a fort at St. Jean gave some impetus to Carleton's recruiting. The first engagement, when Indians and Canadians drove the Yankees back to Ile aux Noix, was an encouraging success. But the patience that enabled the British to wait out a siege was not to be found in the native of Canada. The Indians went home to receive the agent of the Americans, and to listen to the caution adjured to them by their old French leader, Louis St. Luc de la Corne. The habitants, their doubts fed by whispered propaganda, found solace in their growing crops and hope in the harvest.

Apathy to the British cause shifted to collaboration with the Americans as the siege drew closer around St. Jean and the rebels infiltrated north of the fort. The farmers of the Richelieu Valley sold their produce and their cattle to Yankee buyers. James Livingston, so well connected with the Livingstons of the Hudson, was able to raise troops among his neighbors on the Richelieu. These habitants, many of them veterans of the French war against England, were useful to the Americans as soldiers, bateaumen, and gunners. Even Moses Hazen, who rushed to Carleton at the onset of war, had second thoughts and was now raising a regiment for Congress. In the dark kitchens of the habitants, Ethan Allen was able to whip up the Canadian farmers into cursing the English. That he coupled their tacit agreement with his own enthusiasm caused the catamount of the Green Mountains to boast to General Montgomery that his followers among the habitants were legion. More quietly, the American officers spread over the land. Colonel Bedel held the lower works at the crossroads where the St. Jean-Chambly road turned toward Montreal. John Brown walked that road at will with his Massachusetts men. Lieutenant Colonel Warner of the Green Mountain Boys roamed even to La Prairie and Longueuil, where he could see Montreal across the wide St. Lawrence.

In the city, General Carleton held loyalty by the force of his own personality. He commanded a wavering loyalty among the militia. The seigneurs and the Church held to the British who, in the person of the governor, had been fair to their old culture and their faith. But Carleton was not strong enough to force the martial law on dissident English-speaking merchants and the malcontents among the French. Thomas Walker and his noisy ilk still walked and talked in the streets of Montreal. Valentin Jautard flaunted his radical ideas in freedom.

Convinced by his own bravado, flattered by his small following of Connecticut volunteers, and encouraged by

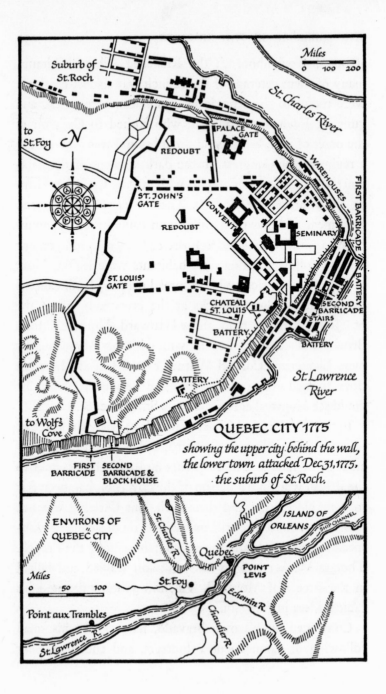

Miles
0   100   200

Suburb of
St. Roch

St. Charles River

to
St. Foy

N

PALACE
GATE

REDOUBT

WAREHOUSES

FIRST BARRICADE

ST. JOHN'S
GATE

CONVENT

SEMINARY

BATTERY

REDOUBT

ST. LOUIS'
GATE

SECOND
BARRICADE
STAIRS

CHATEAU
ST. LOUIS

BATTERY

BATTERY

BATTERY

*St. Lawrence
River*

to Wolf's
Cove

QUEBEC CITY 1775

*showing the upper city behind the wall,
the lower town attacked Dec. 31, 1775,
the suburb of St. Roch.*

FIRST
BARRICADE

SECOND
BARRICADE &
BLOCK HOUSE

ENVIRONS OF
QUEBEC CITY

St. Charles R.

ISLAND OF
ORLEANS

SHIP CHANNEL

Quebec

POINT
LEVIS

Miles
0   50   100

St. Foy

Echemin R.

Point aux Trembles

St. Lawrence R.

Chaudier R.

Walker, Jautard, and St. Luc de la Corne, Ethan Allen set out to capture Montreal. As at Ticonderoga, Allen's dream of taking the city was his own precocious child. General Schuyler, who had employed Allen with reservations, and General Montgomery, who employed him as an *agent provocateur*, were unaware until too late that once again the big frontiersman was following his independent way. Major John Brown, however, was at hand with the same sure sense of opportunity that had brought him to Fort Ti in time for Ethan Allen's great adventure there. Brown had at his back two hundred men, including many of the Green Mountain rangers. Allen had eighty men of what had been a much larger force.

The two men met on the road near Longueuil. For the duration of their talk together, Brown believed in the great scheme to capture Montreal. By the time they parted, Brown to launch his attack from the west, the lawyer-soldier from Massachusetts began to have doubts. At La Prairie, where the St. Lawrence is very wide, Major Brown called off his attack.

Ethan Allen, who had recruited thirty "English Americans," crossed the river from Longueuil during the night of 24 October. As at Ticonderoga, it required three trips to get his army across. At sun-up, Allen was in position east of Montreal with a scout, listening for Brown's signal: three cheers in unison. He waited for two hours. Still no signal from Brown, nor was there any word from Thomas Walker, supposedly poised to cause confusion in the city. With only a hundred and ten men, even a man as dauntless as Allen hesitated to attack a city. Without enough boats he could not retreat across the river, so Allen withdrew to the east and chose a likely spot to await the return of messengers, sent to rouse his allied commanders to bold action.

The British force sent out by General Carleton found Allen and his men in a complex of farm buildings, hay ricks, woodpiles, pens, and picket fences. There were about five hundred British under a Major Carden, brought together that morning when the alarm was given. Coming on the rebels in the early afternoon, Carden's Indians, Canadians, and Loyalists slipped easily into a position for a fire fight. The few British regulars, older men of the headquarters garrison, waited for orders and kept their breath. Ethan Allen, sword in hand, took the initiative. With a flourish, he sent out a detachment of Canadians to flank the enemy firing line. The habitants, who were earning fifteen pence a day, deserted. A second group, sent around the other flank, deserted, too. Allen, with only forty-odd men around him, withdrew. In spite of the wounded, they made good time toward the river. The lumbering old regulars were soon outdistanced. Only the Indians, the Canadians, and the British officers could keep up a running fight with the fleeing Yankees.

There was a moment when a British officer got a clear shot at the broad back of Ethan Allen. He missed, but Allen was forced to take cover. He fired back, also missing, but sending the Britisher diving for a safe place. Each from his own hiding place, the two men reloaded, fired again, and opened shouted negotiations for surrender. Allen was moving back after each shot by the Englishman, who in turn was moving forward from tree to tree as he could, calling terms the while. Finally they agreed, and Allen, dropping his musket, stepped out into clear view. Convinced of honor intact and assured of quarter for his men, Ethan Allen, holding his sword by the blade, stepped confidently into captivity.

General Carleton's victory was not in the skirmish and the capture of the hero of Ticonderoga, but in the triumph when the prisoners were led through the city. The whole town saw the stunned men shamble through the streets ahead of their wounded comrades in country carts. Though there were only a meager twenty-eight captives, all knew by the size of his deeds and his stature that the big man was Ethan Allen of the Hampshire Grants. The Indians of Caugnawaga saw him, and sat down with St. Luc de la Corne to reweigh the balance of their loyalty. Thay-en-da-ne-gea, the refugee leader of the Mohawks and respected man of the Iroquois, saw Ethan Allen humbled in captivity. Under his English name of Joseph Brandt, the Mohawk chief accepted Governor Carleton's invitation to go to London and to see the power and might of Britain. The two men sailed together for England on the last fleet of the year, the Indian an honored guest, Ethan Allen in shackles with his men.

General Carleton took the moment of British success to beat the recruiting drum through Montreal and its environs. Nine hundred habitants answered its triumphant roll. At last, Carleton had enough men to answer Preston's ever more urgent appeals for help for St. Jean. On 30 October, General Carleton embarked his force to cross over the St. Lawrence to Longueuil, there to begin the march to the Richelieu.

From a clump of bushes, Lieutenant Colonel Seth Warner saw the British boats draw near to the south shore. Out of sight behind him, the crew of the little 4-pound cannon crouched, the drag ropes ready, the piece loaded. Along the shore, watching the incoming boats, two hundred Green Mountain Boys and some Yorkers of the 2nd Regiment hid and waited. In the silence of their lines, they could hear the squeak of tholepins and the voices of boat captains giving the final orders for the run in to land. On a shout from Warner, the gun crew ran forward. The musketmen began their aimed fire all up and down the riverbank. The gun fired and the little splashes of grape-shot freckled the water around one of Carleton's boats. Someone in the boat screamed, a scream heard above the shouting and the splashing of the oars. The American musket fire was deliberate and sharp, as the cannoneers went through their drill of reloading. There were a few scattered shots from the boats, turned about now and drawing away. The little cannon spat once more, but the British were well out in the river, bound for home.

Again, Montreal was defenseless. Remembering the harvest, the habitants went to their farms. The Indians, too, had preparations to make for the winter. Carleton and his few British, loyal Canadians, and a band of Scottish-Americans of Colonel Maclean new regiment were alone in Montreal. Across the river and over the flat St. Lawrence

plain, Major Preston waited in Fort St. Jean for the help
that did not come, for the seemingly reluctant winter, for
the Americans to go away.

Major Preston and the garrison were alone on the Richelieu River. Twelve days before Carleton tried to get
through to St. Jean, the fort at Chambly had surrendered.
For three days the honorable Major Stopford in his stout
stone fort withstood the trifling cannonade of the guns that
General Montgomery sent down the river. On 18 October,
the major concluded his timid defense and hastened to surrender before the magazine blew up, the Canadians broke
in to rape and plunder, and all the other imaginable hor-
rors might occur. For John Brown and his Americans, the
surrender of Chambly fort was a haul: arms, ordnance,
military stores, food, and ships' rigging filled the casement
rooms. In his haste to save himself and his garrison, Major
Stopford had left everything neatly stored and catalogued.
But best of all, perhaps, were the eight British officers, the
seventy-six men of the 7th Foot, and the hundred women
and children. These were displayed in a long miserable
procession past the walls of St. Jean.

The British officers of the garrison crowded the parapet
of St. Jean to see the prisoners walk by. None returned the
salute of the faint-hearted Major Stopford. The officers
of the fusileers turned away when their regimental color
passed in the hands of the Yankees. As the straggling group
of women came opposite the gate, three of them detached
themselves and walked toward the fort. At the partially
opened gate, three British officers waited to be reunited
with their wives and end their anxious separation.

The storm that rode the edges of a Caribbean hurricane up into Maine, where General Arnold was marching, fell on St. Jean as icy, wind-driven rain. It chilled besieged and besiegers alike. To Fort St. Jean it brought sickness. Fewer guards could be found, and the damp, stinking cellars of the battered barracks were crowded with the wretched and the sick.

Hope still stood by the lonely sentry, watching through the bleakness of the drizzle. He had heard the news that the Indian brought: five thousand British soldiers had landed in Canada and were coming to their rescue. The sentry could also detect the smell of roasting pig. From somewhere, somehow, nine pigs had come running across the field toward the fort. They had been admitted and caught, and were now roasting all in a row. When his relief came, the sentry would have the piece he knew had been saved for him.

But a messenger who was less cheerful than the Indian and pigs soon came to St. Jean. He was a Montreal hairdresser whom the officers knew, and knew to be periodically insane. The man came under a flag of truce to tell Preston that Carleton had indeed been turned back; no five thousand men had come; and General Montgomery would accept the surrender of a most honorable enemy. Major Preston sent the mad hairdresser away as an unreliable witness.

Richard Montgomery was closing in. The dilatory old General Wooster had finally arrived. The Connecticut troops had turned docile when their own general had come, and meekly accepted the New Yorker's right to command. Also, General Montgomery finally had gotten his landside battery. It had been built from Bedel's north camp, to play on the northwest bastion of St. Jean. The damage to the fort, broken palisades, holes in the barracks roof, earth slides down the walls, was very apparent now, and told the watching Americans that the garrison could no longer keep up with the repairs. While the guns continued to play on the fort, General Montgomery pressed forward his campaign of diplomacy. Under a second flag of truce, he invited Major Preston to send an officer to question a gentleman of substance from Montreal, held prisoner in Montgomery's camp.

John André, dressed in his best coat of red and blue with a clean ruffled stock at his throat, went out to meet the unknown Montrealer. They met alone in the cabin of the sloop *Enterprise*. André heard the worst. On his return to the battered fort and the staunch British soldiers he made his report to Major Preston, who opened negotiations leading to the surrender of St. Jean. On 3 November, the British garrison surrendered. Wooden-faced, John André walked proudly between the odd ranks of the Americans, some in uniforms of blue, some in green, the most part in civilian clothes and remarkable as soldiers only by their "strength, stature, youth and ability." André carried in his mouth his dearest possession, the little miniature of his lost Honora. He had expected to be stripped and robbed by the wild colonials.

The fall of Montreal followed ten days after Major

Preston's surrender. The short march across the plain from St. Jean to the St. Lawrence was agonizingly slow behind Brigadier General Wooster, whom Montgomery had complimented with the lead. But even that old campaigner could not have moved faster. More rain, more snow fell to erase the road, churned deep in mud by the rolling wheels, stamping hooves, and marching feet of the American army. Montgomery crossed the St. Lawrence in a gale of wind on 12 November. The next day, the Connecticut contingent led the army in a formal parade into the conquered city.

Even before St. Jean's fall, General Montgomery was planning ahead to the fall of Montreal and his march to Quebec in support of Arnold. At Sorel, north and east of Montreal, the St. Lawrence River is joined by the Richelieu. Here the channel of the great St. Lawrence is split by many islands which choke its entrance into wide Lake St. Pierre. To Sorel and the narrow passages of the St. Lawrence, General Montgomery sent Colonel James Easton. The man who had stood with Brown against Arnold at Ticonderoga sailed down the Richelieu from Chambly with guns and men in captured boats. He arrived too late to capture Colonel Maclean and his highlanders, who had come from Montreal and made good their escape to Quebec. Easton was joined at Sorel by John Brown, and the two Americans quickly emplaced their guns and made batteries on both banks of the St. Lawrence and on the islands between. Their mission was to stop the British boats, trying to escape the inevitable capture of Montreal.

Guy Carleton had eleven boats in the fleet in which he tried to make an escape from his doomed city. Into the

THE GARRISON OF THE BESIEGED

eight cargo boats he had crowded stores and the one hundred and thirty soldiers that remained to him. Some were on the two armed gunboats as gunners. The governor himself rode on the *Gaspé*, and with him went the revolutionary merchant, Thomas Walker, a prisoner at last.

The fleet of little boats got away on 11 November. They passed successfully the American battery just building on Ile Ste. Helène and came to Sorel, where an adverse wind prevented them from running the American batteries there. While they waited for the wind to change, Major Brown rowed out under a flag of truce. From the deck of the *Gaspé*, Brown pointed out the American artillery covering all the approaches. In the grand battery at Sorel, whose fascines could be seen from the bow, were two big 32-pound cannon, or so John Brown said. He was believed.

After the American left, Guy Carleton made his decision and laid his plans. The little fleet must be abandoned; he himself must get through to Quebec. Carleton knew from his Indian spies that Benedict Arnold was coming over the Height of Land. Colonel Maclean had gone to Quebec to co-ordinate the city's defenses with the city's governor, Hector Cramahé. The governor must follow, to make his stand against the rebels in the last corner of Canada that remained to Britain.

In the night, an open boat came and lay alongside the *Gaspé*. Heavily garbed rowers sat quietly on the benches. In the stern at the tiller sat Captain Bouchette, of one of the sloops. The "Wild Pigeon," as Bouchette was called, knew the river, and he could get the governor through the island passages, past the *Bostonais*, and into Lake St. Pierre.

Soon Guy Carleton came. His dress was as much a disguise as protection against the bitter cold of the night. He wore a woolen cap and a heavy blanket coat, the latter bound around the waist with the customary sash of the habitant, the *ceinture flèche* of Canada. One of the oarsmen helped the governor down into the open boat. The last they heard of him aboard the *Gaspé* was the faint rubbing of well-greased leather on the tholepins and the drip from the oars as they were carefully carried forward for the next stroke.

It was dark on the river, and cold. The governor took his turn at the oars until the warmth of exertion stilled his shivering, and the hands in the mittens no longer were numb. At a grunt from the "Wild Pigeon," the *voyageurs* shipped their oars and brought out paddles. They moved more silently now, with the loom of the islands more felt than seen in the darkness around them. For a time, they floated down with the slight current in utter silence. When the "Wild Pigeon" could feel no movement under the boat's keel, he whispered one short word. Obediently, his men turned slowly in their seats and with bare hands stroked the boat through the cold water, out into the current again. There was no sound in the boat and none came from shore. A faint lapping against the side of the boat told those aboard that they were through the narrow passage. The paddles were brought out again, and once more the men breathed deeply. Soon Captain Bouchette ordered out the oars. Another half-hour, and the rowers began the song, the gay nasal chant of the French-Canadian *voyageur*, the song that is emphasized by the chunk of the oar dropping into the water, and the grunt as the pull begins. The

"Wild Pigeon" had flown through the night; the important Englishman was safely away. There were girls and there was brandy in Quebec City, where they were going. The siege could begin, once they were there with their good governor, the brave General Guy Carleton.

11

The Wall of Quebec

Before Carleton could get there, the fall or the stand of Quebec City depended upon a Frenchman and a Scot, both of whom shared with the governor a common background of service as officers in the British army.

Hector Theophile Cramahé was born in England of French parents in 1720. He had come to North America as a mature captain of the 15th Foot, for the siege of the Fortress of Louisbourg. General Wolfe had noticed him and the following year had employed Cramahé on his staff as a judge advocate, a position in which his French heritage could best be used. He first entered Quebec with the victorious British Army after the battle on the Plains of Abraham. He remained in the city as secretary to General James Murray, the pacifier, whose understanding and respect for the Canadians helped to smooth the transition from French to English rule. Governor Carleton appointed Councilman Cramahé lieutenant governor for the time that he, Carleton, would be in England drafting and lobbying for the Quebec Act. Cramahé was still lieutenant governor when Benedict Arnold descended the Chaudière River to threaten the city from the heights of Point Levis.

The fruits of fifteen years of labor seemed about to be swept away, as Lieutenant Governor Cramahé met with the chief men of Quebec on the evening of 12 November 1775. An impossible march had brought the incredible *Bostonais* to the river wall of the city. It was a feat that could only have been achieved by the wolf packs of the forest—or by men that were wolves. In a day or two the *Bostonais* would be across the river, prowling the city wall and marauding in the suburbs. To keep the Americans outside the walls, Cramahé had but seventy British soldiers, heirs of the armies of Wolfe and Murray. There were some English sailors from the vessels winterbound at the anchorage in the lower town. There were a few gunners and artificers. But the mass of the defenders would have to be from the untrained militia, which was divided into two regiments, one French-speaking, one English. The town leaders who met with the lieutenant governor were grim-faced and resigned to a peaceful surrender to the menace of Benedict Arnold, whom many of them knew. At fifty-eight years of age, Hector Cramahé faced his third siege of the city that had become his home, and whose people were his friends.

Allan Maclean, as Scottish as heather and as tenacious as a burr, burst into the room where the gloomy council was meeting. He came from off the river, where a storm was blowing up rain and snow and angry, white-capped waves—a storm that kept Benedict Arnold's canoes bound to the south shore. Maclean came from Sorel with a hundred men of the Royal Highland Emigrants, and he came to

Quebec only hours after another one hundred and thirty men of his regiment had arrived from the recruiting ground in Nova Scotia.

The Emigrants were like their colonel, Scots of the old highland regiments, the Black Watch, Montgomery's, and Fraser's, who had taken their discharge in North America. At the call of Allan Maclean of Mull, son of Maclean of Torloisk, the highlanders had come to march again to the skirl of pipes. There were many more of them than the two hundred and thirty who came out of the storm on 12 November. The outbreak of the rebellion had caught them far from either of the two rendezvous set by Maclean at Montreal and at Halifax in Nova Scotia. The two hundred and thirty who answered the roll-call in Quebec City were the most hardy and the most lucky. With these good men at his back, Colonel Allan Maclean decided the wavering council of the lieutenant governors to hold fast to the city that Wolfe had besieged and that Murray had defended, in both cases with success.

Arnold's thirty-odd bark canoes lay overturned and stacked on the riverbank while the storm abated and the waves subsided. Sentries watched over the precious craft and patrols kept sight of the British ships' boats, watching and cruising in the river's chop. Other men of the army that had marched from the coast of Maine kept busy with preparations for the quick assault on the nearly defenseless city. Some made the long, strong ladders by which the stormers would scale the city wall. In Arnold's army, which had no cannon, every fit man would be a stormer in the surge which would carry them over the wall and into the streets beyond. The fifer, Caleb Haskell, and a party were marched fourteen miles to where there was a forge, well stocked with tools and iron. Haskell, who was a cabinet-maker by trade, worked at fashioning and fitting the sturdy shafts to the spearheads, hammered out on the anvil, tempered in the sizzling tub, and ground sharp on the grinding wheel. The boarding pikes would be useful at the top of the ladders and in clearing the walls of defenders.

On Monday, 13 November, the day after Maclean and his highlanders had arrived in Quebec, word went out to the Americans to assemble at the mill above Point Levis. Five hundred men were to cross the river that night; the other hundred and fifty were still too weak from their march for the hard work of the night and the early morning.

At nine o'clock, the first wave launched the canoes. Arnold led in the pilot boat. Daniel Morgan sat in the bows with his rifle ready in the crook of his arm. Dr. Senter sat hunched between two rowers, his saddlebags of instruments and medicines at his feet. Arnold's mittened hand on the bar guided the boat out onto the dark river. The first of the lines of canoes trailed close astern. It was two miles from the mill at Point Levis to Wolfe's Cove and the foot of the road up the escarpment. There were British boats on the river, but Arnold avoided them. The boat touched shore under the loom of the cliff and close by the notch against the sky that marked the way to the top. The cove was deserted and silent. Daniel Morgan found no one in the little house that was there.

Benedict Arnold took the house for headquarters, and

set Dr. Senter to building a fire in the fireplace, in case the house was needed as a hospital. Outside again, the colonel set his sentries, dispatched patrols, and himself helped gather wood for the bonfire which would guide the second convoy to the concentration point. The risk of the fire's alarming the British watchboats had to be taken in order to get the men in, together, and with time to get up on the plains above.

About half-past twelve, Arnold lighted the bonfire. The second wave came in, all but two canoes, one of which was known to have split and foundered. All the men except Lieutenant Steele had been fished out of the icy water. While they were bundled, shivering, into the house where Dr. Senter waited, Arnold stood at the water's edge, waiting for the missing canoe and, hopefully, for Lieutenant Steele, the man who had led the scouts all the way from the lower Kennebec. The canoe finally came slowly out of the dark, dragging the lieutenant like a flotsam log behind it. Unable to climb into the tipsy craft, Steele had locked his arm over the stern and the steersman, ensuring the lieutenant's grip by sitting on his hands, brought him in. They fished him out of the water and ran with him, stumbling, into the house, where the doctor stripped him and rubbed him and trickled strong liquor between his blue and quivering lips. By morning the hardy lieutenant from Pennsylvania was again with his company.

Before the third convoy arrived from Point Levis, a British watchboat came snooping. Arnold hid his men in the darkness and, as Wolfe had done when the French boats came into this same small cove, tried to bluff the British sailors away. But the English, perhaps remembering, were suspicious. They hovered at the edge of the firelight and peered toward the flames. With the third convoy expected, Arnold gave the order to fire on the boat. There were screams of agony and sounds of confusion, which nevertheless faded away out of the light. On shore, the Americans heard the boat making off for Quebec, muskets and pistols on board firing an alarm.

With the element of surprise gone with the boat, the risk of a slaughter in getting over the wall became too great, and Colonel Arnold altered his plans. When the third wave of men came ashore, he ordered them to stack the canoes on land. The ladders, which were to come over on the fourth passage of the river, no longer were needed. Instead, with the five hundred men then on the north shore, Benedict Arnold climbed up the little road that Wolfe had found and had used. As Wolfe had done, so would Arnold: he would bring the enemy out to fight on the Plains of Abraham.

First, however, he marched his men across the plain to the big farm on the St. Foy road leading to St. Jean Gate. The first soldiers to arrive—the riflemen—shared with headquarters the luxury of the big house that belonged to Major Henry Caldwell, who that morning was rousing out the English militia in the walled town. The companies that came later took the sprawling farm buildings for their own. In the gray of dawn, the Americans made a strongpoint of the farm, setting out their guards while the others slept in the haymows and the sheds, or in the luxuriously appointed big house. A party of riflemen went out to watch

and listen along the city wall, among them George Merchant of Morgan's, as sleepy and tired as the rest, unaware
that he was beginning a long, long journey that would take
him, a prisoner, to England where he would be exhibited as
a typical example of the dreaded American rifleman. The
officer assigned Merchant his watch-post and left him. With
heavy-lidded eyes, George Merchant crouched down to
keep his trust. Soon he fell asleep.

Benedict Arnold was awake in the room that he had
taken for his office. There his officers came to confer with
him. Fully dressed and shunning rest, he waited for an encouraging word from his friends in the city. From their
letters, Arnold knew that Quebec City was short of food
and firewood, and that the people were disaffected and
without protection, or had been until the arrival of Maclean. On the morning of 14 November there was still hope
that the gates might be thrown open and the Americans
invited to enter.

About noon, there was a smattering of fire along the
riflemen's picket line, and the stand-to was given at Caldwell's farm. Arnold was on the steps of the big house,
impatient as always, hurrying the companies forward, turning to listen to the popping of rifles, now dying down. On
arriving with his troops in fair view of the city, Colonel
Arnold learned the cause of the commotion. The enemy
had not sortied in force; only a sergeant's patrol had ven-
tured forth, surprised George Merchant, and bustled him
off, a prisoner of war. Indignant riflemen told anyone who
would listen how they had tried to get Merchant back before he was swallowed up in the gate to the city. The men

of the musket companies stood quietly in their ranks, observing the discomfort of the elite riflers.

Half a mile away stood the great wall of Quebec, solid and silent. On the left, it climbed up the tilted land from the tributary St. Charles River and the suburb of St. Roch. The wall ambled along, following the jutting angles of bastions. The heavy gates of St. Jean and St. Louis, formidable structures of hardwood and iron, cut short the run toward the city of two west roads across the plain. On the right, as the American army faced it, the wall climbed up the height of Cape Diamond, where the magazine and the last bastion clung to the very edge of the high cliff that dropped down into the St. Lawrence.

Colonel Arnold had drawn up his troops in company front, facing the wall of Quebec. The ragged troops were themselves a wall of defiant flesh and spirit, set against the stone and mortar of the city's wall. Boldly, impertinently, by their presence on the plain, the ranks of the rebels challenged the king's troops to come out through their heavy gates and fight for the possession of Quebec. Stolidly they stood there, showing all the townspeople behind their city wall that if they did not come out to surrender, no food, no fuel, no commerce could go in.

They stood in silence, those five hundred men drawn up in their line no more than three hundred yards long. They were a tatter-tailed band, those hard-worn men from New England and the back country of Virginia and Pennsylvania. Many were bareheaded, their hats gone in the eddies of the rapids that had overset a bateau on the Dead River. Coats needed patches, and coats were tied around with bits

of rope to replace buttons snatched away by the thick
branches in the tangle around Chaudière Pond. Shoes that
had begun to rot in the shallows of the Kennebec had been
replaced with makeshift bundles of green cowhide from the
beasts slaughtered on the Chaudière. Trousers and stockings were torn, laying naked scratched legs and thighs and
knees bearing scabs from painful falls along the weary miles
of the Great Carry. So they stood in the early afternoon of
the mid-November day, shifting their feet against the seeping cold that was in the Canadian earth and looking with
the confident, appraising eyes of soldiers at the walls of
Quebec, that were at the end of their long journey.

On the American right, where the riflemen were, a few
men moved forward, using the slight folds of the ground
for cover. A few heads had been seen above the wall and
figures moved across the open spaces of the gun embrasures.
Each head, each body, was a target for a well-aimed rifle
if the marksman could but get forward into fair range.
From the little group in the center of the line where Colonel Arnold stood, Major Febiger detached himself. He
walked slowly away from the Yankee line toward the
wall. No sound, no shot greeted him as he walked along
the rock face of the bastion. Then, satisfied with his stroll,
the young Dane sauntered back to where his colonel stood.

Nothing had happened. Nothing happened now. Then,
as the afternoon wore on, Colonel Arnold stepped out in
front of his line so that all of his men could see him. When
all were still and watching, he raised both arms. At the
signal, the whole American line cheered. Again and again
he raised his arms and the five hundred voices sent their

hurrahs rolling against the walls of Quebec. Thus taunted, the British gunners let loose a cannon. The ball struck short, bounded, skipped, and finally rolled dead, well in front of the American line. Other guns, 12-pounders and big 32s, took up the cannonade of the ragged barrier of men who had presumed to cheer. The shots fell harmlessly on to the plain; no one was hurt.

With nothing more to gain, and with the chances growing that a lucky shot would cause an unnecessary casualty, Colonel Arnold gave the order to end the demonstration before the wall. But the impudent little army of Americans had come to the great Canadian city of Quebec, and had defied it.

Somewhere on the two-month, six-hundred-mile journey from the coast of New England to the shore of the St. Lawrence, the American army had lost ten days. At his writing-table in Major Caldwell's big house, Colonel Arnold could not find the lost days in tally. The missing time was in the flooded waters of the Dead River, the wait to cross the stormy St. Lawrence, and in the days that had accumulated in the hundred and eighty miles of wading through the shallows and the rapids and the forty miles of portage trails. What could not be numbered was the fatigue and the hunger that cost cumulative hours for rest. The ten lost days were the difference between arrival at a city demoralized and defenseless, and a city capable of defending itself and willing to do so. During the ten lost days two British ships, the frigate *Lizard* and the sloop-of-war *Hunter*, had come in from the sea to anchor off Quebec.

The highlanders, with their terrible screeching music, had begun to arrive from Halifax and Sorel. Finally, on the ninth day, Colonel Allan Maclean himself had come to Quebec City on the wind of the distant war. Together, Maclean with his soldiers and Lieutenant Governor Hector Cramahé with his civilians closed and barred the city to the five hundred howling Yankees who, on the tenth day, clamored to be let in.

As he marched back from demonstrating before the walls of Quebec on 14 November 1775, Benedict Arnold ceased to be an independent commander of a special task force under George Washington for the Continental Congress. He was a unit commander of General Schuyler's Northern Army, whose field force under Brigadier General Richard Montgomery, as Arnold would hear two days later, had captured Montreal.

Although he had spent all the resources of his army and was destitute of every creature thing, Colonel Arnold still had the bodies of his men and his own audacity with which to fight. Siege operations were begun at once. For the second time, Arnold sent Volunteer Ogden forward to the St. Jean gate to present a demand for the surrender of Quebec. The letter, addressed to the Honorable Hector Cramahé, contained the platitudes usual on beginning a siege. It condemned the "venal British Parliament," extolled the humanity of General Schuyler's army, come to relieve Canada. The words that Arnold wrote promised security to individuals and their property unless he was forced to carry the city by storm, in which case every severity could be expected. All this was writen in the name of the United

Colonies. As young Ogden approached the gate with his
flag held high and the drummer beating the parlay, he was
greeted by musketfire from the top of the wall. Prudently,
the proper young gentleman from New Jersey turned back.
Arnold appended a second letter to the first, protesting the
indignity to the ambassador of the United Colonies, and
asking if it were true that the prisoner of war, George
Merchant, was being kept in irons like a common criminal.
Three times in all, Volunteer Ogden marched bravely up
the St. Foy road, and as many times was driven back by
aimed musketfire. Neither Cramahé nor Maclean, nor the
British captains of ships, chose to recognize as a nation the
self-styled United Colonies. The unfortunate Ogden was
shooed away like a fly annoying a carriage horse. George
Merchant, of course, had been chained like any other wild
creature of the woods.

For six days Colonel Arnold with his five hundred men
kept the blockade. Captain Hanchet sent over from Point
Levis the men who had recouped their health and strength.
Captain Morgan took the riflemen down into the suburb of
St. Roch. There they occupied a big log schoolhouse owned
by a community of thirty nuns whose chapter house, con-
veniently, stood in the line of fire from the northern angle
of the wall. The nuns were Christian and friendly, as were
the habitants who lived all around. There was a trickle of
deserters and political exiles from the city, who brought
Arnold the kind of news that he wanted to hear. One gentleman, who had been banished to his outlying farm, told
the American colonel that Maclean was about to lead out an
attack.

Less certain now, as the city organized and as two more vessels (one reportedly loaded with men) had come from upriver, Arnold made an inventory of his resources. Company by company, the count of arms and ammunition came to his desk. The total showed that of the men's muskets and rifles, one hundred were dangerous to fire and beyond immediate repair. When the kegs of cartridges were broached, their contents was found to be damaged. Of all the cartridges that had been rolled on the Dead River, there were but five left to issue to each musketman.

Faced with a sortie and with no means to repel it, after taking counsel with his captains, Colonel Arnold withdrew his close containment of Quebec. Early in the morning of 19 November, while it was yet dark the American army decamped, marching through thickly settled country to Point aux Trembles, twenty miles upriver. The march was quiet and peaceful, past many handsome churches where blackrobed priests stood watching in the doorway as the *Bostonais* passed by. Captain Mathew Smith's rifle company was trudging along close to the water's edge as the two British vessels passed, bound downriver for Quebec. The first was an armed snow, the second a big schooner, both scudding fast in the swift current. The riflemen all turned their faces to stare at the sight of the hurrying ships. In the *Fell*, which was the first to pass, Guy Carleton peered long at the marching column of soldiers. In their faces, in each man's carriage, in the march discipline of the whole, as well as in the direction which they were going, might lie the clue as to whether or not Quebec was still in British hands. Carleton could not be sure until the guns of the city boomed their answering signal to the *Fell* and continued their firing in a long, joyous salute to their returning governor.

The welcome that the guns of Quebec gave to Carleton was heard twenty miles away at Point aux Trembles. In the riverside village the men from the Atlantic colonies were finding their billets in the houses of the habitants. They read aright the message of the distant guns that Carleton had come, but they scarcely heeded it, intent as they were on the soldiers' work of making themselves comfortable.

Since Sartigan, they had become familiar with the ways of the French Canadians, their strange habits of eating and drinking and living, and their stranger, idolatrous habits of worship. Engineer Pierce was able to admire the life-like, life-size figure of a crucified Saviour as "a very striking resemblance," and the reticent Major Meigs of Middletown, Connecticut, dined at headquarters with the parish priest of Point aux Trembles. As for the habitant, he shrugged and was very philosophic toward the odd customs of the heretic *Bostonais*. It was of no importance that the ravenous Mr. Henry chose to eat at each meal enough beef to suffice a family for a week. The cattle were there in the wintering sheds, and the officer from grand headquarters paid promptly in hard money. As with all civilian populations visited or occupied by a liberating or conquering army, the price of beef went up.

Colonel Arnold himself kept the key to the war chest, which by the time it reached Point aux Trembles was virtually empty of silver and gold. There was paper money, but the habitants were skeptical of it. Only three months be-

fore, Benedict Arnold had been called to account for the
pounds and pennies he had spent to "buy" Ticonderoga and
the fleet that controlled Lake Champlain for the summer
and autumn of 1775. He had been careful to the point of
miserliness of the monies that Government gave him, with
which to bid for Quebec City. Arnold had stinted on the
purchase of the men's food since crossing the St. Lawrence.
Some of the captains had resented his niggardliness. In a
stormy interview at Caldwell's house, Morgan and Hendricks and the outspoken Smith had demanded that the
chest be opened and the good things be bought for the men.
Strong words and their implication of flagging morale got
the army their extra rations, but there was not the money
to give the men their back pay. Again Benedict Arnold ex-
ceeded his budget; again he offered his own credit for the
good of the service and the succor of his men. He spoke of
his need for cash in the letter he wrote to General Montgomery, dated at Point aux Trembles, 20 November 1775.

For the soldiers, the days of waiting for Montgomery to
come with all his might were days of holiday. The sentry,
standing in the increasing cold of the November nights,
passed his warm coat and blanket on to his relief and went
into a comfortable billet to drink his hot broth before
seeking his bed by the stove. In the daytime the off-duty
soldier watched or plagued the cobbler, making his new
pair of winter moccasins. Arnold had found a cache of
furred seal-skins, and had rounded up all who had the skill
to fashion footwear. The days passed in luxurious idleness.
The men noticed that the snow which fell was winter snow,
remaining on the ground. They tested the ice forming

along the shore of the St. Lawrence, and there came a morning when it would bear a man's weight a few rods out from shore. The men were like runners at a village harvest feast: they had been first to touch the goal—the walls of Quebec. Now they waited near the finish line for the second runners to come up, so that the next game of the day could begin. For Benedict Arnold, the race was not over. He was keeper of his team, and as a colonel, he was a member of the general's team coming now from Montreal.

For Colonel Arnold, each day of waiting meant long hours at his desk. His friend and secretary Eleazer Oswald was with him. In the anteroom where his staff worked, the young volunteers were on call to run errands and to carry messages. Mathias Ogden was the first to go to General Montgomery with the headquarters mail. From a rankless cadet, Ogden was promoted captain. Three times he had been exposed as a target from the walls of Quebec. He was entitled to the local rank of captain, and to the trip to Montreal.

Arnold wrote openly to his general in the manner of an accomplished soldier to a respected commander. He congratulated Montgomery on his victory and explained, without apology, the reason for the withdrawal to Point aux Trembles. A previous letter, believed lost with its bearer, had accounted for Arnold's failure to take Quebec. Writing on, Benedict Arnold gave his estimates of the enemy force in Quebec, and his own opinion that two thousand men would now be required to carry the town. If the general could spare him six hundred men at once, Arnold could cut the city from its supplies. The cannon (and in respect to the thick walls Arnold recommended mortars) would of course be slower in coming down from Montreal.

To his letter, Arnold appended a list of the warm clothes, caps and stockings, mittens, shirts, and blankets that his tattered men needed so much. He also gave to Captain Ogden letters of introduction and credit to Montreal merchants with whom he had done business in former days. The man standing guard at the door in a stained and torn blanket in lieu of a coat and shirt, and the six hundred others like him, must have winter clothing whether or not the general could supply them.

On the twelfth day after the army of the Kennebec came to Point aux Trembles, General Montgomery arrived. He came sailing down the river in a big topsail schooner, with two smaller schooners following behind like dainty doe trailing their buck. Arnold's men were down on the shore, cheering and shouting welcome to soldiers crowding the decks and yelling back their greetings.

Shortly after noon the honor guard was turned out and marched to the landing dock, where Colonel Arnold and his staff joined them. They were not kept long waiting. About one o'clock the general's boat shoved off from the schooner and headed in toward the land. The guard was called to order. Arnold alone moved down to the shore end of the dock. By rolling their eyes, the guard could watch the crowded boat butt through the fringe ice, and the flurry of activity as the sailors made her fast. They got their first sight of Richard Montgomery when he detached himself from the boat to walk quickly toward their waiting colonel. They got a much closer look at General Mont-

gomery's pock-marked face as he walked slowly down
their ranks, flicking his eyes in quick appraisal of each man,
poised in rigid salute. The honor guard watched, frozen-
faced, as the colonel and then the general introduced their
respective staffs. The names of Captains Cheesman and Mc-
Pherson were new to them but seemed to fit the well-
favored men who bore them. There was no need to say the
name of the tiny young man hovering close to General
Montgomery's elbow. He was now elegant in a fine new
set of clothes, but everyone recognized Aaron Burr. He had
marched with Arnold's army from Cambridge to Quebec.
He had traveled the whole long way with his friend Parson
Spring, the chaplain. It was said in the army that the two
had traveled much of the way with a young and beautiful
Indian girl whom Burr, much envied, had now abandoned.
The men of Arnold's army told of how little Aaron Burr
had carried a message from Quebec to Montreal disguised
as a papist monk, though some said it was as a nun. Now
Burr was back, as well dressed as when boarding a ship at
Newburyport, and as glib of tongue as when he passed
them on the Kennebec in the waist of the chaplain's canoe.
But now he had left their colonel to take service in the
coterie of a general. The official party moved out of the
guards' line of vision, their own stocky, swarthy colonel
in friendly conversation with the tall, fair general. The
honor guard, which had missed nothing, was dismissed. The
soldiers' words of approval of the new general spread
quickly through the old army.

Later in the afternoon the men of Arnold's army saw
their new comrades in arms. They were not the New Eng-

landers like themselves that they had expected to see. All of Montgomery's Connecticut militia had gone home, once Montreal had been captured. Though he had asked them, even begged them, to finish the campaign, their time of enlistment was drawing to a close and they wanted to get back to Connecticut before the real winter set in. Even the men of General Wooster's own regiment chose to go home rather than to stay the winter with their friendly old general in the Canadian city. Montgomery's army that came ashore at Point aux Trembles was made up of New Yorkers, the same mean men who had panicked in the dark woods at St. Jean. They had improved little with service which had neither tempered them in battle nor bound them to each other and to their officers, as had been true of Arnold's men. When led by the tall man who was their general, they might do well in a charge against the great wall of Quebec. As they shuffled about unloading the schooners they looked more like stevedores, which in fact many of them were, than soldiers. They were accomplished only in soldiers' tricks of idleness.

Included also in Montgomery's army was Colonel James Livingston's 1st Canadian Regiment of Continentals. Long in name, short in loyalty, the *congressistes* were heirs to the owl-wise *chouayens*. Best received by Arnold's veterans were the men of John Lamb's artillery company, though to the soldiers who had been at the great wall of Quebec City, the guns that they brought with them seemed puny things. Of the heroes of the Richelieu River campaign, the Green Mountain Boys were markedly absent, as were Bedel's rangers. But Captain Duggan came, ready to chal-

lenge the British on the St. Lawrence as he had done on
his native Richelieu. The darting, secretive Major John
Brown came, too, in the wake of General Montgomery,
and close by him, as always, was Innkeeper Easton and his
small band of western Massachusetts men, who were Lawyer Brown's obedient judge and agreeable jury. Despite
his efforts, Brown had not been made a colonel, in which
rank his nephew by marriage had gained fame and favor
in the eyes of generals. Major Brown now stood distant
from the happy congratulatory meeting of the two armies,
but he found friends to listen to him in Captain Goodrich,
from his own Berkshire hills, and in Captain Hanchet,
who had had Arnold's particular trust.

The day that Colonel Arnold's expeditionary force entered into General Schuyler's Northern Command ended
in the gathering dusk outside of the Church of St. Francis
de Sales in Point aux Trembles. All of Arnold's men were
drawn up, each in his own company with his tried friends
beside him and his tested officer in front. General Montgomery was talking to them. He was speaking loudly, so
that his own men, standing back in the shadows of the
coming night, could hear the praise he gave to Colonel
Arnold and the soldiers who had come with him the long,
hard way to Quebec City. He used the phrase "invincible
courage."

Later, when he was writing his report to General Schuyler, Richard Montgomery called Arnold's soldiers "pretty
young men." They were pretty in the sense of fine, which
is as their general wrote it. They had not been pretty to
the eye as they stood there on parade in the trampled

snow. Ragged and torn, hunched and cold, thin and worn, they were a meager corps of young men who had left their youth on the terrible rivers. In its place they had acquired the posture of men, and a style of discipline that made soldiers of Americans. The general had given them warm clothes and handsome dress in which to display their pride in self and in country. Being soldiers, they cheered Montgomery for his gift.

12

The Army Within and the Army Without

It was bad enough for Captain John Hamilton, Royal
Navy, to be sent into the St. Lawrence River in the contrary month of November. It meant that he and his
28-gun frigate *Lizard* would be ice-bound at Quebec all
winter. It was worse that the army people who ran Canada
expected him, the senior naval officer on the river, to keep
station despite the ice that had begun to form. Further-
more, although the purpose of his voyage had been to
bring reinforcements from Halifax for the Quebec garrison, he was now expected to bring all his sailors, marines,
and guns ashore to help the soldiers defend their city. Captain Hamilton had convinced the army people that it was
imperative to secure the *Lizard* for winter at once, but for
all that month of November he kept the sloop-of-war
Hunter, the snow, and the two schooners on the river above
the town, following and watching the invading army of
Benedict Arnold. In spite of Hamilton's precautions, the
rebels had sneaked across the river through the line of guard
vessels. Since that night, the navy's job at Quebec had

been to prevent that other rebel and traitor, who styled himself "General" Montgomery, from coming downriver from Montreal with help for Arnold. Montgomery's fleet of schooners, prizes taken between Sorel and Montreal, was a naval and supply force that could not be ignored. Of course, they too were concerned by the oncoming winter.

For two weeks, Captain Hamilton kept his squadron cruising between Cap Rouge and Cap Santé, watched the while by Arnold at Point aux Trembles. The ice formed on the shore, and floes came down the channel with the current, harshly scraping the sides of the wooden ships attempting to claw their way upriver. Before the month changed from November to December, the naval vessels were brought back into the safe shelter behind the promontory where stood the city. They were scarcely gone before Montgomery came and made his rendezvous with Arnold at Point aux Trembles.

The four hundred and eighty-five seamen of the naval contingent were a not inconsiderable part of the force of eighteen hundred men scraped together to defend Quebec. Fifty of the men were off merchant vessels; thirty-five were sailors of the Royal Navy and as such were of doubtful loyalty. For the most part the sailors were reluctant victims of press gangs. Released from the wooden walls of their floating prisons, they had a fair chance to escape into the inviting land that beckoned to them. The American propagandists made the most of the circumstances, by overt bombast and covert seduction, to invite the British sailors to desert and to build in the minds of the British defenders a doubt about the sailors' fidelity. Captains Hamilton and Mackenzie, who led their men ashore, were confidently arrogant men in the British navy way. The stone walls of the city made but a broader ship or a wider prison for the sailors. To the sea and city men caught in the press, the land outside the walls was a vast, terrifying wilderness, far more frightening than the familiar oceans. Out there were Indians who were more to be dreaded than the cat-o'-nine-tails or the rope's end of the boatswain and the midshipman. The ship's junior and petty officers were never far away from the sailors keeping their watch stations in the town. A floor for a deck, a jug hidden behind a powder barrel, a friendly tussle with a little *canadienne*, were luxuries unknown on board ship. Even the leniency of small comforts did not weaken the peculiar devotion forged by harsh discipline into the compressed unity of a ship's crew. The British sailors took their guns on the walls of Quebec and into the blockhouses and barricades in the lower town.

Until the sailors came, there had been but twenty-two trained gunners of the Royal Artillery on all the great wall that was the city's first defense. No soldier is more dedicated to his service than the man who handles the guns, and as Quebec organized for the siege, men who had been forgotten and obscured by years of fruitful peace came forward, remembering their service in the artillery of Louis of France. Noël Voyer, whose name linked him to a seventeenth-century governor of Canada, raised the French

gunners into a company of their own and gave them ordnance to man and their own places at the embrasures.

Colonel Voyer had undertaken the command of the
French in the city. He had in all five hundred and forty-
three reliable men, including the company of gunners.
These were organized into eight companies.

There were fewer English-speaking militiamen, and they
drew their muskets and cartridge pouches from the government stores. Major Henry Caldwell commanded them. He
was an heir to the tradition and estate of the immortal General Wolfe, who had noticed Caldwell in his will to the
extent of a hundred pounds. Colonel Arnold's arrival at
Quebec had cost the major all of that legacy and much
more. When Arnold moved back to Point aux Trembles,
his army left Major Caldwell's big house on the St. Foy
road a thoroughly plundered shell. The desecration of the
place by the uncouth rebels made the next loss to Caldwell
a little easier to bear. Governor Carleton ordered the place,
the house and all the farm buildings, burned to the ground.
Tactically, the property was too well located to permit the
reinforced American army again to occupy it as a strong
point.

Governor Carelton had decided to hold out all winter
inside the city walls. The governor had returned to his
capital to the thundering welcome of the guns in salute.
He had wasted little time in quayside ceremony, but had
darted into the narrow little streets of the lower town and
up the steep stairway to the wide squares of the city. Once
again in his own office in the Château de Louis, the governor got down to business. Carleton was pleased with the

way that Lieutenant Governor Cramahé had kept the city against the first shock of Arnold's arrival out of the impassable wilderness, and against the rebels' demand for its surrender. He praised Colonel Maclean, too, for the defense force that he had so quickly raised and organized. The governor and general allowed the congratulatory atmosphere that he generated to spread from his office and to permeate the town as evidence of his own self-confidence.

It was of no concern to anyone in Quebec that one so exalted as the governor could have doubts as to the outcome of the siege. It was important only that no one should suspect that he had such doubts. As a ruler in peace, however, a governor is duty bound to lay his doubts before his distant superiors in a report unobscured by half-truths. As soon as he had made his estimate of the situation, Guy Carleton wrote to the Earl of Dartmouth, Secretary of State for the Colonies.

General Carleton was well aware that, counting regulars, marines, gunners, artificers, and the highlanders, he had but four hundred and fifty-five men accustomed to war. The confident disdain with which the naval officers accepted the disciplined obedience of their sailors was not shared by the soldier-general. The militia was composed of civilians with arms, not men at arms. The English of that ilk could be counted on to be awkward with the musket and shy of both ends of the bayonet. To put a weapon into the hands of a French Canadian was like sharpening the horns of a bull in a paddock full of horses. In his report to the earl, Governor Carleton described the *Quebeçois* as "Foolish People, Dupes of those Traitors." While considering the fate of the city as extremely doubtful, Carleton flattered himself that he could hold out "till Navigation opens next Spring," and "till a few troops might come upriver."

Having disembarrassed himself of his rational and logical doubts, Guy Carleton entered into his preparations for defense with an energy that glowed with confidence. Without compassion or favor, he demolished homes and buildings in the Canadian suburb of St. Roch for the same reason the Caldwell house had been burned. Where the city wall seemed weak, he set the artificers to palisading it. Noticing that the snow was accumulating in the wide ditch outside the wall, he sent men with shovels to remove it. Carleton had spent too many winters in Canada not to know about the great drifts that could build themselves into a ramp against a wall, even as high as the city walls of Quebec. Descending the steep road and the long stairs, the governor and general inspected the two double barricades in the lower town. The barricade under the three-hundred-foot cliff of Cape Diamond covered the narrow path between the rock face and the river that entered the lower town from Wolfe's Cove. The two parts of the other barricade were at either end of a principal street in the lower town itself. The approach to this barricade was from St. Roch, under the wall and the cliff and through a dockland of warehouses. The way was more than a quarter of a mile before a sharp turn to the right brought one face to face with the first barrier. It was a strong position, mounting two field guns. The second barrier was a hundred and fifty yards up the street. It was well loopholed to cover the whole length of the street with intensive musketfire.

As all the windows and doors along both sides of the street had been boarded up, the entire distance between the two barriers was a closed throughway. Should the enemy break through the initial obstacle, they would be in a slaughter pen. General Carleton manned both barricades with naval gun crews and the less reliable militiamen, who would fight best, if at all, from behind close walls. The lower town, which was but a bastion to the cliff and the wall that encircled the city above, had the disadvantage of having water lap its low shores. Once the ice had formed in the river, the barricades could be bypassed, and an enemy could enter by any of the narrow streets that went down to the shore. In that case, the defenses of the city fell back on that steep narrow way up which the general and his entourage of officers climbed, their breath steaming in the December air. A sentry called out the guard as the party reached the top. Cannon were trained on the little group as it passed by the episcopal palace and turned to make the last short climb to the Château de Louis.

From his office window in the château, Guy Carleton could look out on the militiamen exercising at arms. The harsh, loud, frantic voices of the sergeants shouting at their awkward squads, came clearly through the panes. The discordant sounds of the parade ground reached familiarly back into the general's youth as a subaltern on the square. The chant of orders, the rhythmic stamp and shuffle of feet, the slap and thud of musket-butts, had been the orchestration behind all the working years of Guy Carleton, the staff officer. The old sounds continued as the general and governor waited for the siege of Quebec to begin.

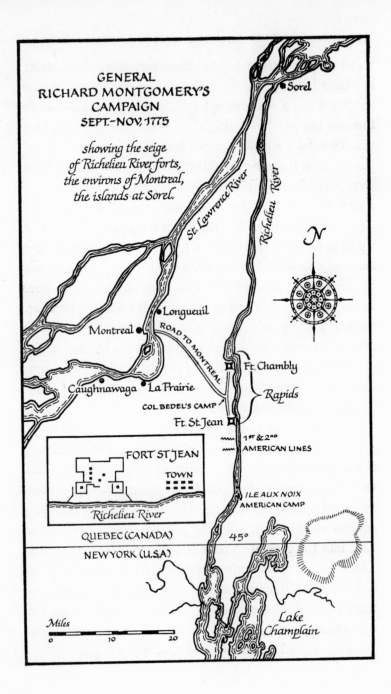

GENERAL
RICHARD MONTGOMERY'S
CAMPAIGN
SEPT.-NOV. 1775

showing the seige
of Richelieu River forts,
the environs of Montreal,
the islands at Sorel.

Sorel

St. Lawrence River

Richelieu River

N

Longueuil

Montreal

ROAD TO MONTREAL

Ft. Chambly

Rapids

Caughnawaga

La Prairie

COL. BEDEL'S CAMP

Ft. St. Jean

1ST & 2ND
AMERICAN LINES

FORT ST JEAN

TOWN

ILE AUX NOIX
AMERICAN CAMP

Richelieu River

QUEBEC (CANADA)

45°

NEW YORK (U.S.A)

Miles

0   10   20

Lake
Champlain

Governor Carleton was expecting the visitor. The Yankees had returned to the wall. Rebel troops were in St. Roch and across the Charles River. Quebec was invested. By custom as rigid as the drill on the parade square, the governer would be summoned to surrender the town. Carleton was therefore expecting the ambassador. He was *not* expecting the old woman who was ushered in to him by the duty officer. From the folds of her shawl the old woman drew a letter, and, saying that it was from the American General Montgomery, she proffered it to Carleton, who was now standing, his desk a barrier between them. All in the room waited on the governor's first word. It came like an echo from the parade square: a sharp call for the drummer. The boy quickly and suddenly appeared. Quietly now, General Carleton instructed the drummer to fetch the fire tongs. The boy did so. Continuing in a low voice that increased only in intensity, Carleton instructed the drummer boy to take the traitor's letter from the old woman, using the tongs, to convey it to the fire and to burn it! The interview was over.

The old woman was escorted to the town gate and sent back to her rebel friends. Before she had trudged a hundred yards through the snow, all Quebec City knew the contempt and disdain in which Guy Carleton held the renegade traitor, Richard Montgomery. In one dramatic gesture, Carleton had set the policy of defense.

Twice more the Americans tried to offer the British terms of surrender. Once, a young woman of the American army came with a letter. She was admitted through the gate, and for two days lodged in the common jail. At the

end of that time she was led back to the gate by which she
had entered. Drummers lined the archway, and to the
scathing beat of their drums, she was driven out like any
mean prostitute. Again the Americans tried to summon
the town. Brigadier General Arnold himself, with an officer
and a man carrying a flag of truce, rode boldly up to the
gate and demanded audience with the governor. Carleton
did not drive the embassy away as Cramahé and Maclean
had done. He merely had someone shout down that he did
not treat with rebels. The city of Quebec was standing,
strong behind its walls and its leader.

On the day after General Montgomery arrived at Point
aux Trembles, the three American rifle companies returned
to the wall. They did not even wait to get the new clothes
that Montgomery had promised them. They moved out by
companies, traveling silently and lightly over the new snow.
They searched the byways as they went, and their track
was like that of the hunting fox in winter, rambling to
right and to left, but leaving the miles behind them. As
they spread out through the countryside in the soldier's
never-ending search for the useful, the curious, or the luxurious, some men of Captain Smith's company found their
way to Lieutenant Governor Cramahé's summer home on
the river. A formidable Irishwoman of immense stature was
the only guard over the place. She made no protest to
Lieutenant Simpson, only glared at the troop of ragged
men tracking snow from their moccasins onto the polished
floor. Being hungry men of a hungry company, the kitchen
larder was the first object of their search. Food such as they

remembered from the Pennsylvania kitchens of their mothers was in the lieutenant governor's kitchen for their taking. The young conquerors filled the wagon they had brought with them with butter, lard and tallow, and beef and pork of the better cuts, both salt and fresh. Returning to the house, the riflemen spread out in the front rooms and in the chambers above. The big Irishwoman watched imperturbably, and from across the room Joseph Henry, with his rifle ready, kept an embarrassed watch over the huge housekeeper. From the upper floor, the soldiers dragged down the mattresses from the beds. In the big chest upstairs they found blankets of a delicate rose color, and from the parlor (when they decided that the sofa was too big for the already overloaded wagon) they took the damask cushions. In the dining room they found cutlery. Perhaps the steel was too finely ground for skinning the hide from a deer or a scalp from an Indian, but the knives and spoons were pretty things, to please some woman at home. Smith's company had been lucky in being the first to find Cramahé's house; as Simpson led his men and the heavily loaded wagon into the main road, a squad of Morgan's men drove up, looking for the house.

There were other places to plunder, and the riflemen found them. The pleasures of a fighting soldier are brief, often crude, sometimes appalling by the standards of a safe life. The loot that Morgan's and Hendrick's and Smith's men took from the absent Tory landlords in the environs of Quebec, they carried forward to places to which no comfortable moralist cared to go. The suburb of St. Roch during the last month of the year 1775 was such a place.

The distant limits of the parish were safe enough. Here the riflemen spent their off day, and here was their second headquarters, in the tavern of Monsieur Minut, or some such name. The officers had been pounded out of their first headquarters by the plunging fire of the cannon on the wall. This middle zone of St. Roch was so dangerous that no American could show himself there in daylight. Even at nine o'clock at night when the new guard went forward, the men moved close to cover lest a coehorn burst catch them in the open. The riflemen respected the skill of the British gunners, who cut their fuses to burst the shells in the air overhead. The third zone of the suburb, where half of the riflemen spent each twenty-four hours, was under the northernmost bastion of the wall. From the bastion a lesser wall, high up on the steep slope, ran east-ward to the palace gate, beyond which were the cliffs and the converging flat land by the Charles River. The riflemen were in dead ground which the cannon could not beat as long as they remained under the bastion and under the wall to the palace gate. In the daytime they dominated the sector with their rifles. A blacksmith shop had been located, which gave enough cover and a good scan of the lip of the enemy parapet against the sky. The British soon learned that it was worth their lives to lean over to see what was going on in the street below. The angle was high for the riflemen, but a treed black bear often climbed as high. At night the defenders rolled mortar shells down the slope. One of these struck and exploded against the house where the off-duty guard from Smith's company slept. The walls shook and trembled, dust and plaster filled the room with a fog, the candle tipped over and went out. There was an instant of panic and aimless rushing about in the low room. Then someone rekindled the light, catching the half-awake riflemen each in his own reaction to fear. No one had been hurt, the solid house had held. The officer, returning from his rounds, found the men talking animatedly to one another in an attempt to explain and excuse their terror. The rose-colored blankets were even paler under the white dust.

Guard duty at night was cold in the suburb of St. Roch. No man could stand for long in the place that he was set. Patrols were better duty, even if they prowled far down the street toward the dockland or walked brashly up to the closed and barred door of the palace gate. But through the long nights of December, whether the sky was bright with crackling golden starlight or the big snowflakes sifted down, or the wet thaw dripped into the slush where the sentry stood, no enemy came to contest the riflemen in the suburb of St. Roch.

From the moment he arrived at Point aux Trembles, Brigadier General Richard Montgomery had given up all hope that Quebec City would humbly open its gates to his summons. That opportunity had gone with the cheers of Colonel Arnold's impertinent gesture. The embassies that Montgomery sent into the city were the merest formalities of law and war. They served, however, as positive acts in that they occupied the time of movement and preparation while the plan for the capture of Quebec matured. The embassies were calculated to sever the precarious loyalty of the cooped-in civil population—which included the militia—from the rooster-like dominance of Guy Carleton.

The governor had countered by three different acts of contempt, which asserted his rule of the roost. By vilifying Montgomery as a traitor, Carleton had increased the respect of the Americans for their general, by defining the line between staunch Whig and despicable Tory. That "Mr. Carleton," as they referred to him in retaliation, had treated a gentle old lady with scorn, had subjected an American woman to humiliation, and had ignored Arnold, the hero, angered the American troops against their enemy. Montgomery could use that anger to kindle fury when the assault carried the Americans into the city.

Even before he had dined and talked with Arnold on the afternoon of his arrival, Richard Montgomery had known that he must fight behind the walls. From Montreal he had written of Quebec that he must "come at last" to storming the place. He well knew the "melancholy consequence" of such an attack. A commander of troops knows the price of purpose and the cost of success. He reads the bill in the eyes of the man who shares his breakfast on the day of battle.

The delegates to the Continental Congress counted with elation the profits and dividends from their investment in their Northern Army. Their generals on Lake Champlain had won for them virtually all the wealth in the whole vastness of Canada. Their Colonel Arnold had plucked a hero's laurel wreath along the impossible forest way. Loudly and eloquently, the men of thought and deliberation demanded that past successes be compounded with the final victory: the capture of Quebec. Then they could truly admit the fourteenth colony to their Union and spend its treasure for the new concepts of freedom and liberty which they were formulating.

General Washington, too, was looking to the "abundance of Canada" to supply the many wants of his army. Ordnance, arms, clothing, equipment, and blankets were needed for the army in Boston. Even as Montgomery and Arnold were meeting, Washington's artillery officer was planning the overland transportation of the cannon taken from Carleton at Ticonderoga and Crown Point. Beyond the lake forts, the long supply line would extend to Montreal and the good farmland of the St. Lawrence. No one in the army or the government or Congress doubted that the Northern Army would soon add Quebec to the tangible assets of the first year of rebellion. Neither General Montgomery nor Colonel Arnold had any doubts about taking the capital of Canada as they stood for a moment together in the snow, watching a company of their soldiers marching in column of route past the church of St. Francis de Sales, on their way back to the wall. They *did* know, the two commanders, that the books of the Northern Army closed with the New Year. At the last stroke of midnight on 31 December 1775, the contract of enlistment expired for most of Colonel Arnold's New Englanders. Unless the men could be persuaded to soldier on into 1776 (and already they were talking among themselves of going home), the Northern Army had only the remaining days of their last month in which to attack the city.

The trouble among Colonel Arnold's troops began in Captain Oliver Hanchet's company and centered upon the captain himself. From the beginning of the overland march, Benedict Arnold had favored Hanchet with his particular trust. When the colonel had needed a reliable, determined officer to dash forward to the French settlements on the Chaudière and bring food back to the starving, straggling army, he had chosen Oliver Hanchet. The captain had performed the extra duty and marched the extra miles back from Sartigan with all possible dispatch. When Colonel Arnold crossed the St. Lawrence on the night of 13 December, he left Oliver Hanchet in command on the south shore of the river. The captain's command consisted of those men still too weak and ill from the march over the Height of Land to make the river crossing and the assault on Quebec, plus the stragglers still trickling down from the sick camps on the upper Chaudière River. When the night proved too short and the Royal Navy too alert to ferry the last wave of able troops across to Wolfe's Cove, those soldiers came under Captain Hanchet's orders. In addition, the reserve stores of ammunition (later to prove defective) and the big scaling-ladders and short spears became Hanchet's responsibility. While the chance to command a hundred and fifty men, 30 per cent of the whole army, was a promotion for a captain, it was gained at the expense of a place in the assault on the city. After a morning of watching and listening from the hilltop of Point Levis, Captain Hanchet knew that Quebec had not fallen. By afternoon, the increased numbers and activities of the Royal Navy boats in the river told Hanchet that he was alone, cut off from the rest of Arnold's army. He was vulnerable to an attack from the river. He was surrounded by French Canadians with whom he had no direct communication and for whom he had a New Englander's inherent distrust. Although at night American canoes ran the river blockade with news, they returned to the Quebec side with the reserves of ammunition, food stuffs, and some of Hanchet's able-bodied men. Daily the captain's independent command was weakened and his vulnerability increased. Nor did an ebullient letter from Colonel Arnold give help or hope to the commander, alone, cut off, abandoned on the nether shore. The letter became suspect, as it said that he, "B. Arnold," would send the boats for all but sixty of Hanchet's men. According to his specific orders from his distant colonel, Captain Hanchet gathered all the leaders and all the stores into the mill, and fussed over the men as they did their work.

The light of Arnold's leadership that impelled men to achieve the impossible of heroism burned most brightly when most challenged. Without the fuel of danger or imminent disaster, the flame faded. The glow was altogether extinguished when it was unrenewed as a result of the circumstances of inaction, or of distances in time and space. As Roger Enos and his captains had lost the inspiration of Benedict Arnold's leadership between the plunging front and lagging rear of the long line of march, so the St. Lawrence River and the hazards of separation quenched the will of Oliver Hanchet to follow his colonel.

Captain Hanchet was disenchanted when Arnold finally fetched him across the river at Point aux Trembles, and the period of idle waiting for General Montgomery began. Reunited with his own company of Connecticut men, Hanchet let his disaffection show. More, he paraded his men to the tavern, treated them all to brandy, and harangued them. As they drank their captain's cognac, they heard Hanchet vow that he himself would lead them back to Connecticut when their time was up. As he reckoned it, that would be four days hence, 2 December. Crowded into the low-ceilinged, hot, foreign room, the men of Hanchet's company drank to their captain, to the month of December, to the second day, and to the Saturday on which it fell.

By the morning of 2 December the mood of drink and boredom had passed. Hanchet's men agreed to stay on with Arnold until February. Little men like twenty-two year old Abner Stocking had remembered in time the firmness and the zeal of Colonel Arnold, who, like themselves, loved his country.

Surveyor John Pierce, a sergeant in the company of his friend Captain Jonas Hubbard, was a man of science, and he wrote in his journal each day. He noted the weather and the wind, the compass bearing and the estimated length of every stage of the march from Maine. At Point aux Trembles, Pierce catalogued the course of the illness that was on him, the purges that he took, and whether or not he was able to turn out for guard. For all his exact science, Pierce was philosophical regarding the things he observed and the people around him. He credited his companions in arms, particularly those like himself and his friends Hubbard and Oliver Hanchet, with being "thinking soldiers." As such, the men of the Congressional army were unique in their world. That their opinions, in agreement and disagreement, were diverse only underlined their individuality.

Oliver Hanchet's disagreement with his colonel took the way of his home colony in smoldering talk and debate which drew other like-thinking men to the right party. Jonas Hubbard and William Goodrich were the captains among them. The leaders of the rifle companies, too, had their disaffection, but like the rifles they cherished they aimed their complaints the direct, straight way. Like a thunder storm in an Appalachian valley, Morgan and Hendricks and Smith had swept over Arnold and inundated him with their demands. And like the sailor he was, Colonel Arnold met them bows on, trimmed sail to logic, veered a point or two to ease the tension, then rode firmly through to reason. All four, the frontiermen and the trader-sailor, were going in the same direction: to Quebec. In one gigantic outburst, Benedict Arnold redirected the riflemen's anger against the enemy.

The "thinking soldiers" of Colonel Arnold's army of the Kennebec were among the loyal and steadfast, too. After Enos dropped out, the field officers of the army quietly continued to do their duty, with a detachment befitting men under a forceful leader. Lieutenant Colonel Greene and Major Bigelow subjugated themselves to their colonel, the former in a manner becoming the son of a judge, the latter with a patience becoming a man who beat tirelessly at the hot iron of his forge until the shoe was made. Major

Meigs, in whose division were Captains Hanchet and Goodrich, avoided controversy. Return Jonathan Meigs merely
performed his duty to the army, and wrote reassuring letters
to his wife in Connecticut.

The captains were more passionate to their duty, to the
cause, and to the objective. Henry Dearborn, who had
given up a medical career to step onto a long, high ladder
of military success as a captain, took sick at Sartigan. The
fever had been growing during the days in the tentacle
swamps around Lake Megantic, but he could not ease his
efforts while he had the Indian canoe and his own men
and the men of the army needed his assistance. From 6
November to 9 December, Henry Dearborn lay sick, de-
lirious at first, later recovering in the settlements on the
Chaudière. In his company it was reported that their captain
had died; someone had seen Charles Hilton making the
coffin. Though he was as weak as water and had to be
helped to stand as he got out of the boat, Captain Dearborn
returned to command his company, then stationed across
the Charles River.

Captains Thayer and Topham remained steadfast in purpose, their men alert, when Colonel Arnold needed them.
Twice, Arnold had to find soldiers to perform duties which
Hanchet refused. The first time was when the ladders and
spears had to be brought over from the mill on the Point
Levis side of the St. Lawrence. Captain Hanchet made so
many excuses, saw so many dangers from British patrol
boats, and protested so vehemently that Arnold dismissed
him. The trip was made by a volunteer company, chosen
by lot. The second time that Captain Hanchet refused as

too dangerous a duty forward at the wall, Topham and Thayer, joined by a molified Hubbard, accepted the job and for three weeks took the pounding of the British guns. At the second instance of "cowardice," all Arnold's fury burst upon his former favorite. Only General Montgomery's wise intervention prevented a court-martial and a mutiny.

Oliver Hanchet was not a coward but a victim of injured feeling, nursed in inactivity, pampered by talk, coddled by rum. Major John Brown provided the soothing lap of sympathy. With his keen nose for opportunity, a prodding finger of revenge on Colonel Arnold, and a foot groping for promotion, Lawyer Brown organized the discontent that he found sulking in the taverns of Point aux Trembles. Within a week of his arrival at Quebec, John Brown had gathered a following and fomented a plot. If Benedict Arnold could not keep his command united, there would be fragments from which to form a new regiment, and Hanchet, Goodrich, Hubbard and his own friend Easton would certainly vote Major Brown colonel over them.

The usages of the New England town meeting, of democracy in detail, was not the way of the Continental army under George Washington, or Schuyler or Montgomery and Arnold. Only Major Brown, whose commission came from a colony and not from Congress, and who stood to gain from his attitude, invoked the selfish right to reject or select authority on a whim. For a time he charmed and stirred the dejected among Colonel Arnold's officers. For a time he mistook as encouragement for himself the complaints among the rankless men. But they, the "thinking soldiers," in giving up their private freedom to the common good and to a high purpose, had reserved their inalienable right to complain. General Montgomery and Colonel Arnold read their soldiers aright as they swung, cursing and grouching, onto the snowy road that led back to the walls of Quebec.

13

The Last Day of Service

Be it cap, hat, or helmet, a soldier wears his pride on his head. Arnold's men wore, like flaunted plumes of arrogance, the little round fur hats that General Montgomery had given them. The general had also brought them the long, warm, white blankets-coats that he found with the hats in the British army stores at Montreal. Underneath this winter garb Arnold's men wore the new red coats, faced with blue or yellow, intended for the 7th and 26th Foot. These, too, were plunder. When a British sentry caught a glimpse of a Yankee on the St. Foy road, or running between the houses down below in the suburb of St. Roch, the man was dressed in a uniform the same as his own. The rifleman looking down the barrel of his long rifle, sighted through the embrasure on an incautious white shoulder a nodding-tailed fur hat that might be his own. Soon, now, the Americans would have to differentiate themselves from their enemy. When that time came, Montgomery would order his soldiers to wear sprigs of evergreen in their hats. Some, in defiance, would pin bits of paper over their brow,

marked clearly with the motto "Liberty or Death." For
all but the last day of December, however, only the line
of the wall drawn across the snows marked the difference
between those within and those without.

Colonel Arnold's wing of the American army outside the
walls held the left of the line. On Arnold's left, James
Melvin and his friend Moses Kimball stood guard. Ever
since coming to Quebec the two had stood guard. The
worst trick had been while the army was waiting for General Montgomery to come down from Montreal. Lieutenant Nathaniel Hutchins commanded the company in the
absence of Captain Dearborn, sick. As Hutchins was the
most junior, he drew the outpost duty. Dearborn's men had
missed all the comforts and pleasures of Point aux Trembles.
They were on the road to Quebec, guarding a bridge,
and the duty at night called for two hours on and
only one hour off. Things looked better for Melvin and
Kimball on returning to the siege. Their company, being
among the first into St. Roch, took for themselves the
nunnery. But the motherly care of the sisters was short-
lived. The colonel found the nuns good company, and Dr.
Senter thought it the right place for his hospital. So
Lieutenant Hutchins and his company were moved out to
the other side of the Charles River, where Dearborn, hol-
low-cheeked, gaunt, and feeble, returned to them. It was
a quiet sector on the low ground between the Charles River
and the big St. Lawrence. The high ground, having let
the tributary river through, rose again east of the city and
was untouched ground for foraging, as well as affording
a fine prospect of the city itself. Melvin could see all the

British ships, secured for the winter, and the marginal ground under the wall and the cliff extending to the little plateau of the lower town. Together, Kimball and Melvin watched the white puffs of cannon smoke which meant that their friends in St. Roch were under bombardment. Sometimes they went into the suburb, crossing on the frozen part of the ice, out of range of the guns. On those trips for sociability or duty (Melvin was on duty in St. Roch the night of 30 December) they saw the damaged walls of houses struck by cannon, and they found, in the most unlikely places, curved chunks of iron flung wide by the bursting shells. These souvenirs they took back with them over the Charles River, and they carried, too, the precious bits of army gossip that they had picked up at headquarters' back door.

The whole army knew the fall of every shot that dropped among them. They knew who was killed by it, who was wounded, who, miraculously, was unharmed. There was indignation when a French girl whom they knew was wounded in the foot, and cheers when refugees came out of the city with tales of the damage the American howitzers had done. Smallpox, probably starting in the camp of Montgomery's New Yorkers, spread to Arnold's men. The rumor that was given credence had it that "Mr. Carleton," the ogre, had sent smallpox carriers from the city to infect the American camp; the story was enlarged upon to include women with the pox.

No official note was taken of Christmas, although the day before, which was a Sunday, Mr. Spring, the chaplain, preached a perceptive sermon in the popish chapel of the

nunnery. He took his text from 2nd Chronicles, and elab-
orated on the strength of the Assyrians being "an arm of
flesh," while God fought for the people of Hezekiah of
Judah. It was a righteous, refreshing sermon, filled with
resounding words. At midnight all the Canadians went to
their midnight Mass and came home happy to share with
the strange *Bostonais* their breakfast of the good pork pie
called *tourtière*. Those soldiers who could do so provided
their own celebrations. Surveyor Pierce and four friends
drank down a quart and a pint of rum, and settled it with
a quart each of sour wine. For a day, the awfulness of their
sickness was the talk of the army.

Underlying the gossip and the scandals of the army was
the vital question of how to assault the town's walls. When
the carpenters were called together to make more of the
long ladders needed to scale the walls, the question became
acute. On Christmas Day the officers were instructed to
poll their men for volunteers for the first stormers. Those
who were against it were loud in their protests that an
assault was foolhardy. They related their chances on the
wall to their chances of going home. The days of the calendar were running out. There was serious talk that, once
the ice had formed on Lake Champlain, Congress was
sending five thousand soldiers, who would soon march over
it and replace the time-expired men at Quebec. Most of
Arnold's men agreed to stay until the relief came. Those
determined to go home saw the frozen lake as an escape
route.

The arrival from Montreal of three hundred more New
Yorkers caused little comment among Colonel Arnold's

men. They had little truck with their comrades in arms on the high plateau of the Plains of Abraham. As for the increase in numbers, the new arrivals scarcely replaced those of Colonel Livingston's *congressistes* who had gone home to the Richelieu.

The only common ground of meeting between the Montreal army and the Kennebec army was the guns. On 10 December, Captain Lamb opened a 5-gun howitzer battery in St. Roch. Most of the staff, in spite of the counter battery fire, gathered in the evening to see the first shell "hove" upon the "Carletonians." The howitzers, however, were but a prelude to the main American battery, building on the Plains of Abraham.

Any thought of digging in the guns was, of course, impossible, the ground being hard-frozen beneath the snow. So during the days Arnold's men and the Yorkers built gabions. This was no easy work, cutting and splitting the wythes with cold fingers, then bending the frozen lengths to weave them into big baskets. At night, carrying parties took the gabions to the battery position, where Captain Lamb directed the setting. Other parties were there, waiting with shovels to fill and pack the baskets with snow. A bucket brigade was organized to wet down the snow, and eventually, after much work, snow and gabions welded themselves into a barricade of ice. Gun platforms were laid in the bays, and Lamb's gunners and the old French gunners who followed Captain Duggan set up their pieces.

All the labor on the battery was in vain. Built at but seven hundred yards from the wall to accommodate the best range for the American 12-pounders, the position was easily reached by the big 24's and 32's that the British brought against it. On the second day one gun was damaged and the howitzer dismounted. The ice wall shattered into cruel splinters and two of the Frenchmen were killed, leaving their blood red on the white snow. Though Lamb had the stains covered, that bay was avoided by the gunners who still came back to fling an annoying salvo at the impervious, defiant wall.

Though he made his feints and opened his battery, these were but gestures by Montgomery to occupy his troops and entertain the enemy with room for doubt. Because of the weather that froze the ground, no digging of siege lines was possible. The ice walls of the battery proved a false hope. Yet General Montgomery intended to use the unfavorable weather to his own advantage.

Since coming to the wall, the weather cycles moving down the St. Lawrence had alternated between clear and very cold, and warm, cloudy days. There had been a day of rain, and on the 17th there was a storm of snow that left all the landscape white again. It turned cold. The natives, who knew the weather, told Montgomery that it was a late winter but that another snowstorm was sure to come soon. Montgomery wanted a snowstorm to mask the cannon and blind the defenders to the rush of ladders and stormers to the attack.

On 23 December the officers of Arnold's wing of the army met in the colonel's house to hear General Montgomery. Almost all were there, crowded together yet separated into groups of fast friends and common interest.

Arnold kept a place beside the fire for the general, who would have a cold ride down from the plain. He came in, tall, handsome, and courteous, remarking politely on the clarity of the winter day—weather which did not fall in with the plans for the attack about which he had come to tell them. Standing casually by the fire General Montgomery calmly conversed about his intent to storm the wall with ladders and pikes. He told the listening officers where they would go over, and he told them where he himself would climb the wall with the New Yorkers. He emphasized the importance of timing and contact in an attack in the gloom of a snowstorm and in the dark of night. The hour of attack was to be synchronized with the next real snowstorm. The officers were to be ready with their men as of now. Captivated by their general's confidence, the officers grew eager, the groups melting into each other like lumps of yellow butter warming on a skillet. Almost casually, without mentioning a name or giving a glance, General Montgomery dismissed any question of forming another command under Major Brown. Colonel Arnold's army of the Kennebec, undivided and united, would put in the attack. In the leaping flame of Benedict Arnold's passion and the hot glow of his angry officers lay the fire that would consume Quebec. General Montgomery asked each captain to poll his men for volunteers to set the ladders and to be first to mount the wall. Other details he left to be explained by Colonel Arnold. Captain McPherson had the door open by the time Montgomery had crossed the room. Together, the general and his aide stepped out into the brightness of the still winter day. Both glanced quickly up at the white-blue sky. Like the officers they had just left, they were looking for the coming storm.

It was warmer on the twenty-fourth, and in the morning it looked like snow. There was a little flurry, but it passed. Christmas and the day after were fine days. General Montgomery used the waiting time to hold reviews and address the troops. Wednesday started out a fine day. A hard snow was falling, whipped and swirled by a gusty wind from the south and southwest, where lay the mountains and the Height of Land. All day the soldiers worked in preparation for an attack at night. Cartridges were checked, bayonets and spears honed, hand grenades issued, fresh hemlock greens and new white paper secured on hats and caps. The ladders were carried up to the start line for the various companies. Patrols went out in St. Roch to get a prisoner who might give the last-minute news from inside the city. One of the parties, from Captain Hubbard's company, brought in an old woman who said that Carleton was building a new breastwork in the lower town. All else was quiet in Quebec. The guns on the wall, masked by the snow, did not fire that day.

If the general was waiting for a storm to cover his entry into Quebec, so were two others in the American camp. One was Sergeant Singleton of the Yorker troops. The other man, named Wolf, who had been a servant at the farm of Lieutenant Governor Cramahé, was captured on the day that Arnold crossed the St. Lawrence. Wolf had been so long a fixture in the American camp that he was ignored. The two now wandered off into the snow. Both knew or had heard enough of the American plan of attack to jeopardize the whole intent.

The deserter and the prisoner were not missed until the night, when the more distant companies were belting on their equipment, preparatory to moving up to the start line. An officer, going in to see the general at his headquarters, noticed that the wind had dropped and that the snow, big flakes, was lessening. Montgomery added this bit of negative information to the certainty that Sergeant Singleton and the man Wolf had alerted the British to his plan of attack. Half an hour before two o'clock in the morning of the twenty-eighth—the hour that the first troops were to move out—General Montgomery went to the door to look at the sky. The snow had stopped falling. The clouds were high, scudding eastward down the wide valley of the St. Lawrence. A star, bright and diamond-clear, appeared for a moment, then winked out of sight. Already a tree not far away was clearly outlined, and beyond, the black silhouette of a house was defined against the new white snow. Soon the clouds would break up entirely and the starlight on the snow would make a blanket of betraying brightness across the plain up to the wall. Turning abruptly, General Montgomery walked into the anteroom where the messengers to units were waiting and gave the order calling off the attack for that night. In a scramble, a snatching of hats, a grabbing of muskets and rifles, the runners bolted for the door. Montgomery was left alone with his decision. The risk was too great, the chance of success too slim. The general must make a new plan, wait for another storm. He had but four days until the enlistments ran out.

The new plan of attack was made during the next thirty-six hours. As in the former plan, the new one depended on surprise, achieved at night under cover of a snowstorm. Assuming that the alerted British would be at the wall, the American general chose an entirely different direction of attack. Where he would have soared over the walls and swooped down on the town like an eagle, now he would enter below, like a ferret loosed underground into a warren. The hole in the basement of Quebec was the steep, narrow way up from the lower town. There were two roads to the foot of the stairs that began the climb to the upper town. Both were long, both were guarded by barricades, both ended in the little streets of the lower town. Reading from his good map of the city, General Montgomery decided to attack the lower town along both roads. He would lead his New Yorkers from Wolfe's Cove, follow the St. Lawrence, under the high peak of Cape Diamond, where the barricades were, to the foot of the stairs. Colonel Arnold would skirt the northern bastion of the wall, pass the the palace gate, and work his way through the warehouses of the dockland. On the map, Montgomery's finger continued to trace the route that Arnold's men would take. The road along the Charles River turned abruptly to the right under the cliff, here called Saut-au-Matelot (Sailor's Leap). Here the British had placed the first barricade. Arnold would need ladders to get over it. At the end of a straight street was a second barricade. Just beyond this last obstacle was the foot of the stairs. Montgomery and Arnold would join forces there. One would await the arrival of the other before climbing up into Quebec behind the walls. With Colonel Arnold, General Montgomery worked out the direction and objectives of each company, when once the American army swanned out through the high city.

Details followed as, step by step, the plan of attack developed. Both commanders personally would lead their men to the place and time of the rendezvous in the lower town. Arnold wanted to take a cannon with him; Montgomery gave him Captain Lamb. Dr. Senter requested that he be permitted to lead a company in the assault. Montgomery and Arnold declined his gallant offer and ordered him to prepare for the reception of casualties in a forward dressing station to be set up in St. Roch. Colonel Livingston and Major Brown were given the task of creating a diversion against the wall. They would make a show of attacking according to the first plan, which was known to the enemy. The signal to start the attack would be rockets set off from General Montgomery's headquarters on the plain. Arnold stationed men so that the signal would not go unseen in the falling snow.

"The last day of service," was the way Surveyor Pierce began the entry in his diary on 30 December 1775. He felt very contrary and liverish that morning, and he had a toothache. Pierce added to his opening sentence "all rejoice, again I say all rejoice." As he had done every day, Pierce noted the weather: "Clear, cold, the wind from the southwest." He was on the sick list, so he had time to note that the weather grew hazy about noon, and spit snow. As the snow fell steadily, Pierce wrote, "The last day of our service, but I hope not of our lives."

At eight o'clock that night men were going around to all the billets, thrusting open the doors to shout that the attack was on. "Be ready at twelve." In the silence the messengers left behind them the stormers of Quebec quietly made their preparations to be ready at midnight.

It was two o'clock in the morning before the men were called out of the warm houses where they had been waiting. Colonel Arnold stood under the cover of a shed, a lantern hung from a beam casting a dull light on the paper Captain Oswald held in his hand. As the captains came up to report their men present, Arnold's secretary checked them off on the paper. Captain Lamb reported in, then wandered off to where his 6-pounder, mounted on a sled, was waiting in the street within sight of the shed. The little crowd of twenty-five stormers under command of a lieutenant was further down the road toward Quebec. One by one, the captains of the Kennebec army, the famine-proof veterans, reported present. Lieutenant Colonel Greene and Major Bigelow, who would command the main body, came up and joined Arnold. Hubbard, Thayer, and Ward came to the sled, saw their names entered, and moved off to join their troops forming the line. Lieutenant Steele stepped into the light and reported Captain Smith's company present or accounted for. Archibald Steele was a bold, resourceful leader of scouts and a good officer. He was poor at dissembling. He had tried to awaken his captain, but without success. He had left the old ranger fast asleep, sprawled across the top of a table. On his own initiative, Steele had brought the company on. Arnold acknowledged the lieutenant's command of the company and he withdrew out of the light of the lantern.

Daniel Morgan, whose Virginians were to lead the main body, reported, loudly as ever, and the rest, too, came into the light of their colonel's glance. Only Henry Dearborn had failed to answer. Word was passed up and down the column waiting in the snow. No one had seen him, or his men. It was getting on to four o'clock in the morning and time to start, when the sergeant major admitted the messenger sent to alert Dearborn who had not been able to cross the Charles River. The sergeant major was sent at once to get Captain Dearborn. Benedict Arnold gave orders that Dearborn, the most conscientious of his officers, could follow on and catch up with the army.

Rockets, one, two, three of them, arched up into the thickness of the snowy night. Arnold could see the glow in the direction of St. Foy as he heard the shouts of his watchers on the high ground. He dashed out of the shed. Lamb's gunners were already leaning into the harness attached to the gun sleigh. The stormers had stopped flapping their arms and stamping their feet as Arnold came among them like a bobcat springing into a covy of grouse. They snatched up their ladders and spears and followed after their colonel.

On the Plains of Abraham, Major Brown's men saw the signal and slowly picked up their ladders. There was no urgency about their task. Livingston's men were excited in their Gallic way. They argued and shouted at one another as they picked up their bundles. Someone forgot to light the torches. The man was sent back to the house, where the big fire lighted for that purpose burned bright. In little groups, the Canadians walked toward the St. Jean gate. A gun fired dully from the wall, then another and another. One by one fire baskets took flame, the bright patches of yellow light showing the wall in all its height and strength. The British artillery now began to pitch fireballs in the rear of the advancing Americans. Though they fell into the snow, they burned and cast into silhouette the men between them and the wall. The British were alert and ready for the Yankee attack.

Richard Montgomery could not see the fireworks on the wall. He was halfway down the road to Wolfe's Cove, under the high loom of the palisades. No longer was he the general who had planned the whole attack. He was the commander of a unit of that attack, with a rendezvous to make at the foot of the stairs. As he reached the shore and turned east on the river road, he could hear the church bells, all the church bells in Quebec, tolling the alert: To arms! The attack!

The urgency was for speed. There were wind drifts of snow under the cliff, and at the water's edge chunk ice made walking there impossible. General Montgomery, with his aides, McPherson and Aaron Burr, forged his way through the deep snow that covered the road. Close behind came Captain Jacob Cheesman with the pioneers, carrying the ladders and their axes and saws. Further back, in the darkness, followed Colonel Campbell. He and his New York troops, divided into three battalions, were making slow work of it.

General Montgomery was at the first palisade about six o'clock. No one challenged him. He walked up to the big pickets and when the axmen came up, he indicated with a pat of his mittened hand which ones he wanted them to cut. Four posts were felled inward and rolled aside. The second palisade barred the road a hundred yards away. Still no one challenged, no enemy fired. A drum beat an old, remembered call on the bastion, high and remote, far above Montgomery's head. The bells still tolled in the city, and small bells clattered far ahead beyond the palisade, where lay the lower town.

General Montgomery chose two pickets off the road under the cliff. Close behind the second palisade was the blockhouse, with its big naval cannon covering the space between it and the barricade. By selecting pickets at the end, Montgomery gave the British gunners an awkward angle of traverse. He took a saw from one of the pioneers and himself cut the two trunks. With his two aides and Captain Cheesman crowding behind, General Montgomery stepped through the narrow opening and moved out into the space between the blockhouse and the palisade to let more pioneers come through.

No challenge came from the squat, ominous-looking building in the road, though a dull light showed the curve of a cannon poking out of a gunport in the upper story. There were men inside the building, citizen-militia of Quebec and sailor-gunners from the ships. Most of the militia had already run out of the back door, frightened by the sawing through of the pickets. The sailors upstairs were leaving, too, in a mounting rush of panic. One of them stopped at the head of the stairs, rushed his way back and grabbed a glowing linstock. He had been drinking. Carefully, he held the match to the priming powder heaped over the touchhole of his gun, which was loaded full of grapeshot. The moment was as long as ages, while the erect sailor stood in the empty room, waiting for the powder to ignite. The gun roared, bucked back, and the flash lighted the room. The drunken gunner tumbled down the stairs and fled out into the night.

In front of the smoking muzzle, General Richard Montgomery lay on his back; close behind lay McPherson and Cheesman, and behind them, two pioneers. The pattern of their bodies on the snow was an arrowhead pointing toward the blockhouse to which they had been running when the gun went off.

Minutes later, Colonel Campbell stepped cautiously through the gap in the pickets. He saw Aaron Burr, dazed but unhurt, wandering dully about. The surviving pioneers huddled in a leaderless group, as far away from the five bodies as they could get.

The colonel from New York scarcely glanced at the dead general. He did not look at the silent deserted blockhouse. He did not see the empty open road stretching away to the lower town. Quickly, Colonel Campbell grabbed Aaron Burr by the arm and hurried through to the safe side of the barricade. The pioneers trailed after them, anxious to follow someone, anyone. Hurrying faster now, Campbell fled through the first barricade. There his battalions waited, and he quickly turned them around and led them back the way they had come.

Colonel Campbell was as empty as the void he left behind the second barricade, as dead in spirit as his general was to life. The road was open into the heart of the lower town. On it, forsaken, lay the bodies of Richard Montgomery and his four comrades. The silently falling snow soon laid a soft white blanket on the upturned face of the American general.

Across the tip of the Quebec peninsula, under the northernmost bastion of the wall, the storming party led by Benedict Arnold broke trail through the new-fallen snow. The colonel took his turn in the lead, dragging his leg through the snow and out, swing it forward and lunging into the next tsep. His broad and strong shoulders swung lurchingly with each forward step. There were heavy drifts where the wind off the St. Lawrence River eddied the snow under the steep cliff banks. The main body of Arnold's troops, the men who had made the march from Maine, would have easier going in the track of the stormers.

Arnold stepped out of the trail to let a fresh man lead. Captain Lieutenant Wool's battery of howitzers was now firing. Arnold had passed by the gunnery officer shortly after the march began. He could hear the big British guns booming up on the wall. A cresset basket of fire on the bastion lighted the straight edge of the masonry high above his head. Up there, a drum beat an unfamiliar call. The church bells, all the church bells in Quebec, were ringing.

The firing from the wall began after the advance party, with the gun sled still at their heels, had passed the palace gate. The musketfire, mixed with tossed grenades and bomb shells rolled down the slope, fell on the main body strung

out in single file. Some of the men were hit. They lay in
the snow, moaning, calling out or cursing as their companions hurried by them, away from the overhead fire.
Beyond the palace gate the extension of the wall ended,
but the fire from above onto the American soldiers continued. The British were following along the cliff, annoying, harassing those they could not see but knew were there.
They were encouraged by an occasional cry of pain.

Around the first corner, where the attack force came to
the shore, lay the warehouses and dockyards of Quebec.
The land was narrow, but it was wide enough to confuse
the direction of the American line and break it. Some companies, turning right around a looming great shed, entered
blind alleys and had to turn back, grumbling, and try again.
There were saw pits and drydocks to fall into, and some
did fall, including Volunteer Rifleman Henry. There were
ships' timbers buried under the snow to trip over, and
overturned boats in drifts to run into. Along the river edge,
cables from the moored boats ran to bollards, and the
houses on shore made a crazy web to catch the wanderers
in the dark. Even the guides who knew the place became
lost, and Natanis himself, the good Indian from the Dead
River, strayed in this wilderness of snowbound industry.
Daniel Morgan, who had intended to take his riflemen out
onto the river ice in order to flank the first barricade, gave
up that intent among the warehouses. There was something
reassuring about the land and the man-made walls of buildings that kept the soldiers of Virginia away from the ice.
The river was silent black nothingness, where the wind
raced, where somewhere the water began, and where the

snow covered cracks and airholes with a terrible carpet of
false assurance. The musketfire from the cliffs inland was
a better chance than out on the dark St. Lawrence. Daniel
Morgan made his way through. He was still leading the
army of the Kennebec. A soldier held Morgan's belt at the
back, another behind him, then another, and yet another.
Still others attached themselves to the long chain of men
forming behind their captain. Morgan passed Captain Lamb
and his gunners, struggling hopelessly with the sled. Lamb
and his men joined themselves to Morgan's line, abandoning
the useless gun. There was light scattered firing not far
ahead. Another chain of men was converging on Morgan
from the other side of a warehouse, with Captain Thayer
leading it. A few steps further on, a little group of men
showed up as dark blobs against the snow. A few more
steps, and Morgan could see that the men were gathered
around a figure seated in the snow. The seated figure was
trying to rise, but his companions were urging him to stay
down.

The figure which finally rose up out of the snow was
that of Benedict Arnold. With the storming army, he had
suddenly come against the first barricade. The enemy had
been alert, and in the first fire from the loopholes a musket
shot had taken Arnold in the side of the left leg, just
above his moccasin. The colonel had gone down heavily
and awkwardly. The pain was no more than that of a
sharp blow, but Arnold could not stand. Some of the men
dragged him back out of the line of fire, and when Morgan
and Thayer came up, Chaplain Spring was examining the
wound. From the warm blood on the chaplain's hands it

was obvious that the wound was bleeding profusely. Spring urged Arnold to remain seated, to lie down, but the colonel had to get to his feet lest the soldiers see him down and lose heart. He was standing, still supported by the chaplain, when Daniel Morgan came up to him. Quickly, Colonel Arnold told the captain where the enemy was, what had happened, and how best to attack the barricade. Morgan plunged on through the snow. As the riflemen and Thayer's men hurried past, they saw Arnold standing, supported by a soldier, while someone knelt at his feet cutting the boot and legging away from the wound. Their colonel was urging them on, as he had so often done on the dread rivers. He was cheerfully promising victory, as he had promised them food when they were hungry. The voice encouraging them in the darkness was the same strong voice that had encouraged them before, when the mile ahead had been so hard. They went ahead, and the sound of American muskets and rifles grew strong and steady against the barricade. Then Benedict Arnold allowed himself to be helped to the rear, where the doctor was waiting. Samuel Spring and a big soldier went with him.

The cold of the air and the sting of the snow on his bared left shin stopped the bleeding, but Arnold had lost a great deal of blood and was weak. At times on the long walk back through the warehouses the little group of three stopped, while the dizziness and the faintness passed. Benedict Arnold was dragging his left leg, now numb, when near the palace gate he met Captain Dearborn and his company, hurrying forward in the track of the army. The colonel sent him on, urging speed on the captain who needed no urging, fearful lest the enemy be all beaten before he arrived.

The palace gate was still closed and barred. Captain Duggan came out from behind a building, and seeing that it was the colonel, reported his Canadians all in place, watching. As yet, no Englishmen had tried to come out of the gate. Several other soldiers, all of them wounded, had passed by on their way to the hospital.

The darkness of the night still covered Arnold as he passed under the north bastion of the wall. Dawn light was coming on, and the ruined houses were taking gray shape. It was almost seven o'clock. Two hours earlier the musket ball had ricocheted off a rock and struck Colonel Arnold in the leg. They brought him into the hospital at first light, but something of him they left at the first barricade, in the spirit and the will of the soldiers he had led so far.

Leadership came naturally to Daniel Morgan. The assumption of the right to command was part of that ability to lead. Though he was only a captain and a lieutenant colonel and two majors were somewhere about, Morgan gave the orders. First, he directed his riflemen to fire at the loopholes and win them. They did so, and Morgan brought up the ladders. They were waiting under the two cannon whose embrasures he had located, cut in the top of the 12-foot pickets. A group of men running forward tempted the gunners to fire. When they did so and the guns were empty and helpless, the scaling ladders were swung up. Captain Morgan was first over the top. In jumping down onto the gun platform he slipped, fell heavily, and was dazed. By the time he was up again, other men with pikes had won the enemy guns, and Americans were jumping down to get at the enemy behind the barricade. In minutes it was over, prisoners rounded up, the gate cleared of snow and swung open. Morgan did not wait for the other companies to come up; he had wasted enough time at the first barrier. Dawn was not many minutes away. With the men he had, he moved down the long corridor of the narrow street. Half-way down its length, a company of French militia came out of the houses, their hands held high above their heads, shouting *"Vive la Liberté!"* Morgan sent them back as prisoners. In one of the houses he found their drunken captain. Morgan's men also found the Canadians' muskets, good new English army pieces, dry and warm to the hand. Quickly they exchanged their own wet and useless arms for the English ones. Further down the street they came to the second barricade. Like the first, there was a gun platform above and loopholes below, but no one fired, and the wicket gate stood ajar. Beyond, the short street was empty.

For a moment Captain Morgan hesitated. He had very few men. Behind him were over a hundred prisoners with insufficient guards. The main body of Arnold's men soon would catch up with him. He stepped through the wicket gate and listened. The steps to the upper town were around the next corner. There was no sound of firing in the distance. Montgomery would be coming very soon.

On the front side of the barricade, the other companies were coming up. Colonel Greene and Meigs and Bigelow were now there, conferring in the darkness of a doorway. They had decided to wait in the houses for General Mont-

gomery to arrive. Daniel Morgan had lost his command to
rank, and his impetus in a moment of indecision.

They awakened Guy Carleton shortly before four
o'clock on the morning of 31 December. There was no
risk in this, either for the duty officer who made the decision or for the valet who actually touched the shoulder
of the sleeping governor general of Canada. For three
nights, the defenders of Quebec had been expecting the
rebels to attack, and Carleton, as commanding general, had
ordered news of any occurrence to be brought to him at
once. Captain Malcolm Fraser was reporting that his highlander sentry on Cape Diamond had seen unusual lights in
the lower town. They could be guide lights, set out by
traitors to beckon a rebel attack force in off the ice. Carleton was getting into his clothes when the three rockets went
up over St. Foy. He was fully dressed and in the street when
the illuminating fires lit all along the city wall. He was in
the Place des Armes, at the spot where all knew he could
be found, as the church bells pealed. Quickly the Place des
Armes filled with the units of soldiers designated as the
mobile reserve of the commander in chief.

The veteran British general waited patiently in the snow
for the reports to come in. At first, all the reports came
from the great wall facing the Plains of Abraham. The
Yankees were making a show of advancing with ladders; a
party was on the St. Foy road, and appeared to be carrying
faggots and torches. The general could hear the guns firing
on the wall and the explosion of an occasional shell from
the rebel battery in St. Roch as it fell in the city. A later

report from Captain Fraser noted that the Americans were not pressing the attack across the plain. It could be a diversion.

The general waited. He ordered the units in the square to march around it in turn, to warm the men up a bit. Then musketfire was heard from the direction of the gate opening toward the old intendent's palace, on the shore of the St. Charles River. A messenger from that quarter soon arrived with the intelligence that a large party of men could be heard passing below in the direction of the warehouses and the lower town. Captains Lawes of the engineers and MacDougal of the highlanders were directing blind fire down on these people. Some minutes after five o'clock, a highlander from the Cape Diamond bastion reported that a cannon shot—only one—had been heard from the blockhouse at the foot of the cliff. There had been a flurry of musketfire, then silence, where stood the first barricade at the opposite end of the lower town, under the rock known as Saut-au-Matelot. The last word from Captain Fraser was that the rebels were still demonstrating, but no longer were they showing any interest in attacking the wall or the St. Jean gate.

From all these careful, detailed reports, the rebel direction and intent was clear. Montgomery and Arnold were attacking the lower town. General Carleton could now move his reserve to defend the stone steps and the steep way up, should the rebel army win the barricades and, as they would have to do to gain the city, assault upward from below. Carleton did not at once send men down into the lower town. Even with the best-trained troops, to control and concert a counterattack at night—and such a dark and stormy night as this—was a military impossibility. The soldiers he had could hold a firm position even at night, but would panic in the melee that is street-fighting in the dark. There was yet an hour before first light. After an hour, the musketfire at the first barrier at Saut-au-Matelot had ended with a single cannon shot. Silence had followed, and as no firing came from the second barricade there, the assumption was that the first one had held.

Anxious about that single cannon shot at five o'clock from the Cape Diamond blockhouse, General Carleton sent a small force to strengthen the forty-eight Canadian and English militia and sailors holding it. On their way down the road the men met and shoved their way through the crowds of civilian refugees escaping from the lower town. None could give any clear account of what was happening below.

The dawn was not far off when Carleton sent orders to Captain Lawes and two hundred men to sortie out of the palace gate. They did so, brushing away Captain Duggan and his *congressistes* like so many flies on a sugarbowl. Turning right into the tracks left by the passage of Arnold's men through the snow, Lawes caught up with the rear of Captain Dearborn's company. Lost and wandering among the warehouses, Dearborn surrendered. Captain Lawes lost some precious time in getting the dejected prisoners back through the palace gate. Hurrying now through the morning light, the hazards and pitfalls of the dockland were gone. Lawes found, looked at, and passed by Captain Lamb's gun sled, overturned and abandoned. That bit of booty could wait. Cautiously now, Captain Lawes approached the first barricade. He could see its entire hundred-yard length of tall logs, reaching across from the base of Saut-au-Matelot Rock to the river battery on the dock which he knew as Limeburners' Wharf. No one was at the barricade. The gate was open and many tracks led through it. Captain Lawes halted his troops to wait. Some walking wounded came out of the gate and were taken prisoners. One man saw the British in time and ran away; the Yankee army would soon know that their line of retreat was closed.

With the full light of day, General Carleton sent a strong patrol down into the lower town to locate the enemy. The force was a mixed one of sailors and Canadians, including some seminary students, and highlanders and fusileers of the 7th Foot. The leading element went cautiously down the stone steps and in among the buildings. Carefully turning each corner, eyes searched the windows in the upper stories. Lieutenant Anderson, of the Royal Navy, found the Americans in the street between the barricades and stepped brashly through the still-open wooden gate, calling to the rebels to surrender. Daniel Morgan, who was in the street, flung up his rifle and fired. Lieutenant Anderson staggered back through the gate and fell, shot dead through the head. Quickly the gate was slammed shut, and the Canadians under Captain Dumas manned the barricades.

Caught in the open, the Americans took heavy casualties. Dumas and some others had scrambled up and onto the gun platform, and were trying to load the piece. On the American side, Captain Morgan was bellowing up an assault. His fight developed into a personal one with a huge Canadian

THE LAST DAY OF SERVICE

above the picket wall. Morgan had put up a ladder. Charland, the Canadian, was trying to pull it in before the rifle captain could climb on to it. Charland won, and the ladder arched up and over, to disappear inside. The cannon fired, raking the narrow street. The Americans, running, stumbling, dragging their wounded, ran for the shelter of the buildings. The dead were left where they had fallen, among them quiet Captain Hendricks, huddled against a wall.

There were windows and doors at the back of the houses. Some of the Continental officers tried to lead sorties that way, but fusileers and highlanders were there and drove the Yankees in with well-timed volleys. All grew quiet where Carleton's men watched the street and the houses where rebels were trapped. At the far end of the street, Captain Lawes and two hundred men waited at the other barricade.

The American officers knew Lawes was there. Some talked of fighting their way back, others wanted to go forward, most were content to stay where they were. Some watched idly as Lieutenant Steele, the scout, tied a handkerchief over the stumps of three of his fingers that had been shot off. None cared to look toward the bed on which lay Captain Lamb, moaning softly. They had all seen the shattered and bloody pulp of his face; there was no eye at all in the torn and gaping socket.

The heat of battle cooled. Benedict Arnold, their leader for so long, was gone; General Montgomery had not kept the rendezvous. All animation had been drained from the privates, who waited patiently for their officers to do something.

At ten o'clock on the morning of 31 December 1775, Lieutenant Colonel Christopher Greene surrendered for them all. Including Captain Dearborn's company, four hundred and twenty-six officers and men were made prisoners. Perhaps sixty had been killed in all the action of the morning.

Without arms, they filed out of the houses into the light of the day. Files of Canadians indicated with their muskets that the Americans were to go through the wicket gate toward the stairs, and so, finally, into Quebec City.

Daniel Morgan still showed defiance. He backed against a wall, and with the sword he was to surrender, glared across at the row of muskets challenging him. Tears ran down his powder-stained and bearded face. His bullet-torn hat was askew on his head. Then Morgan's red-rimmed eyes shifted to where a priest was standing, and to him Captain Morgan gave his sword in surrender.

Already the British doctors were entering the buildings to tend the American wounded.

Dr. Senter found the ball in Colonel Arnold's leg and neatly extracted it through an incision he made opposite the point of entry. Both the surgeon and the colonel were surprised to see that the ball was only two-thirds of its original size. But it had passed between the two bones of the lower leg, both of which had been chipped, cracked and bruised, and muscles had been torn at the top of the Achilles tendon. The colonel would probably walk with a limp for the rest of his days. Now, pleaded the doctor, would he please go to bed and remain there for eight weeks. Major Ogden had just come in with a shoulder wound that needed attention.

The major brought discouraging news from the lower

town. He had little hope of success. From the plain, news soon came that Montgomery was dead, and the others with him. Colonel Benedict Arnold, flat on his back, again was in sole command of all the American troops investing Quebec. With only a hundred or so of his own "hunger proof veterans" left, there were a scant eight hundred men in the American army before the city wall. These included Livingston's and Duggan's unreliable Canadians, John Brown's independent band from Massachusetts, and the New York troops who, with their colonel, had run away that morning. In his bed, with the pain in his leg growing more intense, Arnold contemplated turning over his command, in strict protocol, to the despicable Colonel Campbell, he who had left his general's body to lie forsaken in the snow.

Calling for pen and paper, Benedict Arnold wrote a hasty first report to General Wooster, the senior Continental officer in Canada. Arnold lay flat on his back. There were so many reports to write: to Wooster, to Schuyler, to Washington, to his sister Hannah, at home with his children. He would urge Congress to send five thousand troops—that number would be needed to hold Quebec City, once it had been taken—and cannon, big cannon to batter the city into submission. Washington must send a general, a good general. Old Wooster, who drank in public taverns with jailors and butcher-boys, would not do. Arnold would ask that Major General Charles Lee be sent as the man finally to conquer Canada. In the west of the great continent, the forts at Niagara and Detroit had not yet been taken. Already, Benedict Arnold was riding a fast horse into the future of his imagination, a good horse which recognized neither failure nor obstacle.

In the afternoon, Dr. Senter appeared in great alarm. British troops from the city were out, roaming the plain, and were in the suburb of St. Roch. Captain Lieutenant Wool had thought best to withdraw his battery of howitzers, and was setting them up to defend the magazine from marauding bands of habitants, now unfriendly to the Americans. Senter implored Arnold to let himself be moved into the country, to avoid capture. Benedict Arnold ordered all the wounded men in the hospital to be issued muskets to defend the place. He called for his brace of pistols, and laid them to hand on the counterpane. In distress, the doctor left him ready to fight on.

But the British did not come to the hospital where the wounded colonel slept. General Carleton called all his men back within the walls behind which he was so content to stay, and where he and Canada were safe. There was a victory to celebrate that night, and the birth of a New Year. For Colonel Maclean's Scottish soldiers it was Hogmonay, the grandest holiday in all the year.

Epilogue

MAJOR GENERAL RICHARD MONTGOMERY

As Overseer of Works for the garrison of Quebec, James Thompson had much to do at the blockhouse and barricades under Cape Diamond on the morning of 31 December. Several of the big logs forming the palisades were reported to have been cut and cast down by the rebels in their attack. Thompson was there early to assess the damage and order repairs to be made at once. He also supervised the removal of the bodies of the dead Americans. The snow had continued to fall and had covered the bodies so that they were but hummocks, like so many graves in a carelessly laid out cemetery. From one of the mounds an arm upthrust into the air. They dragged the body out from beneath its covering, and Thompson saw that the man was an officer, apparently one of rank. There were three wounds in the body. One bit of grapeshot had entered the head through the chin, one was in the groin, and a third had shattered the thigh bone. A drummer boy scuf-

fing through the snow found the officer's sword. James
Thompson snatched it from the boy as something too precious for a mere drummer, though later he gave the lad
seven shillings for his find. The sword was a hanger type,
short-bladed, ivory-handled, with a bulldog's head pummel
of silver. Many British officers of wealth affected similarly
worked swords.

With his loot in his hand, James Thompson saw the bodies carried into the guardroom. Later, a cart hauled them
up into the dead house, or vault, where bodies were kept
until the spring thaw. In the cold room, where lay all the
American dead, an effort was made to identify the owner
of the silver sword, and two people from Quebec identified
the body as that of Richard Montgomery. The Widow
Prentice, who kept a hotel where Montgomery had stayed,
recognized a scar on the cheek. Lieutenant Governor
Cramahé, too, recognized in the dead face the man he had
soldiered with in the old war. Finally, to make the important identification positive, Governor Carleton had an
American field officer taken prisoner at Saut-au-Matelot
view the body. There was no doubt that General Richard
Montgomery, in the forefront of his attacking men, had
been killed by the single cannon shot.

Montgomery was buried with dignity in Quebec City.
He was a major general when he died, having been promoted by Congress on 9 December. He was mourned by
his former comrades in arms, whom he had forsaken for
the new call of Liberty. James Thompson, who supervised the details of the funeral, afterward wore Richard
Montgomery's sword as his own.

BRIGADIER GENERAL BENEDICT ARNOLD

Neither shock, pain, nor immobility kept Benedict Arnold from exercising command over the remnants of the American army outside the walls of Quebec. He had succeeded to that position on the death of General Montgomery. Just after the doctor had extracted the broken ball from his leg, there had been a moment when Arnold temporarily had turned over the command to Colonel Campbell. Then Colonel Arnold had been told the details of Campbell's timidity after Montgomery had been killed—conduct for which Colonel Campbell later was court-martialed. Benedict Arnold's judgment and determination as a bed-ridden cripple were better than those of Campbell on two strong legs, so quick to run away. Arnold took back the command and for two months ran the army and the siege of Quebec from his sick bed.

Most of Colonel Arnold's work during the months of January and February consisted of writing letters. This he did lying flat on his back, then propped up by bolsters, then sitting in a convalescent's chair. The letters were written with the same fury with which he rode a horse, the precision with which he sailed a schooner, and the certainty with which he led men into danger.

Benedict Arnold showed no vanity of rank or conceit of military prowess, that winter of 1776. In accepting and admiring Richard Montgomery, he had recognized the ability of a trained and experienced professional soldier to organize and conduct a military campaign. When Arnold wrote to General Washington in mid-January, he asked that Major General Lee be sent to Quebec. Like Montgomery, Charles Lee was a former British officer, and at the time Arnold wrote, was field commander of the troops besieging Boston.

In writing directly to Washington, Colonel Arnold was committing the cardinal military sin: going over the head of an immediate superior. But Arnold had urged Brigadier General Wooster, senior officer in Canada, to come himself with troops and complete the capture of Quebec. David Wooster remembered Benedict Arnold as the impetuous young captain of foot guards, who, on the opening day of the rebellion, had mutinously seized the powder stores at New Haven, when he, General Wooster of Connecticut, was responsible for them. No one in command above him had authorized Wooster to give powder to Arnold. No one —neither Schuyler at Albany, Washington at Boston, nor the Congress at Philadelphia—had authorized Wooster to go to Quebec. The old veteran in his third war was not inclined to accept the urging of a colonel so junior to him, particularly one who had risen so rapidly from a captain of militia to a Continental colonel, while he, David Wooster, had gone down in rank from major general of Connecticut to brigadier general in the army of the Congress. Besides, the number of troops at Quebec were scarcely consonant with the dignity of his generalship, and Montreal was a congenial place for a man of his age to spend the winter. Brigadier General Wooster did send a colonel and one hundred and sixty men to Arnold as a token.

The Congress and General Washington were more helpful. Immediately on hearing the news from Quebec, the

Continental Congress resolved to reinforce the "American Army in Canada," and within the week had a Jersey battalion and a Pennsylvania battalion marching toward Quebec. John Hancock, president of the Congress, wrote to Washington asking him to send a battalion from the army at Boston. The president also authorized Washington to importune the governments of Massachusetts and New Hampshire each to raise and send a regiment to the Northern Army. General Washington could not send General Lee, on whom he depended. In March, however, he sent the best of the new generals: John Thomas had distinguished himself at the siege of Boston, and had earned his promotion to major general.

But as of 10 January 1776 there was a general officer at Quebec. On that day in Philadelphia, Congress made Benedict Arnold a brigadier general in its service. Crying for help like a hound with a coon up a tree, Arnold pressed his siege of a defiant Quebec. Wounded and unable to lead his men, with his own army of the wilderness march all gone, and left with only eight hundred indifferent Yorkers, Canadians, and militia, General Arnold could not again assault the walls. All he could do was to contain the city, while preparing a tighter and tighter investment as each new contingent arrived at his camp. When the new general arrived, the army would be ready and in position for the final attack.

Always short of artillery, Arnold found his own supply of guns. There was a forge and foundry at Trois Rivières, and the ironmaster, M. Christophe Pélissier, was able and willing to cast mortars and shells. With these and Lamb's guns as a nucleus, Arnold set up a battery on the Plains of Abraham, across the Charles River, and on Point Levis. From the high windows of their jail in Quebec, the American prisoners watched the incoming shells from these batteries.

There was smallpox in that jail, and in the city, too. The disease spread to the American camp, and it met the soldiers coming up from Montreal on the last leg of their long winter journey from the Atlantic seaboard. While Dr. Senter's hospital filled with new patients, the old wounded from the attack of 31 December returned to duty. By March, Arnold was up and about the camp, limping about with the aid of his stick, or riding on horseback to the distant batteries.

On 8 March, the Pennsylvania battalion began to arrive at Quebec. By the end of that month fourteen hundred new troops had joined Arnold. The Americans appeared to be winning the race to reinforce their army. Governor Carleton had yet a month to wait before he could begin to expect the troops that he had asked England to send him.

The movement of fresh American troops through Montreal stirred General Wooster in his hibernation. Optimistic reports from Arnold's army at Quebec roused the old general from his contented slumber. The sweet maple sap of spring was in David Wooster's old bones and a taste of victory on his lips as, in late March, he hied himself down the St. Lawrence to Quebec. Being six months senior in grade, Brigadier General Wooster could claim the command of the Quebec army from Brigadier General Arnold. This Wooster did, with a particular lack of grace and no acknowledgment of his junior's tenacity, which since November had maintained the siege of Quebec and by April had brought it to a peak of expected success.

The day after General Wooster arrived, April Fool's Day, Benedict Arnold waited upon the new commander. Unfamiliar officers had the run of the new headquarters as Arnold waited to be admitted. His own officers, Greene and Meigs and Morgan and Dearborn, even Hanchet, all were prisoners in Carleton's jail. In prison, too, were the men he had led through the wilderness to stand, cheering, outside the walls of Quebec. His friend Richard Montgomery, whom he had so much admired, was also within the city walls, lying in his grave. Alone outside the walls, Benedict Arnold waited for General Wooster to see him.

The meeting between the two brigadier generals was brief and formal. Arnold pleaded his wounded leg, aggravated by a recent fall with his horse, and asked to be relieved of all duty. Brigadier General Wooster was sympathetic but urged his junior, on his recovery, to take command in Montreal, a most healthful and important city.

Benedict Arnold departed Quebec as precipitously as he did most things. All his plans and preparations he abandoned to Wooster, to use or misuse as that officer saw fit. Arnold was riding west to Montreal with new hopes and with some doubts. Far to westward, two British forts dominated the trade routes from the Indian lands. One was at Niagara, the other at Detroit, leading to the upper Great Lakes. Both places were worthy of the attention of Congress, as Arnold had pointed out in a letter written as long ago as 12 January. In Arnold's field desk, as he went down from Quebec to Montreal, were sketches and notes for boats suitable to maneuver and fight in narrow waters. These vessels, three-gunned gondolas and row galleys from the inland Mediterranean Sea, could easily and quickly be built for a Great Lakes navy. They also could be built to defend Lake Champlain, should the British come in strength and chase old General Wooster out of Canada by the way he came. Like Ticonderoga, like St. Jean, the Height of Land and Quebec City were of the past. Arnold was moving in a new direction, off on a new tangent of adventure.

For a month after Benedict Arnold went away, Brigadier General David Wooster, with considerable pomp, maintained the siege of Quebec. Including the few remaining squads of the Kennebec army, General Montgomery's New Yorkers, those companies that during the winter had come to Canada over the frozen roads, and the Montreal troops that had come as his escort, Wooster had in all two thousand soldiers under his command. The number was impressive when, broken down into units, the roll was read to the general each morning as he made a good breakfast in his comfortable headquarters. The weakness of the army could only be seen from a closer scrutiny of the men who made up the army. Although five hundred additional troops arrived during April, only nineteen hundred remained on the rolls when May Day came. The hardship of a long winter of service was showing its effect on the health and will of the soldiers. Death from disease and epidemic thinned the ranks. Without decisive, purposeful leadership the morale of the troops declined. The rate of desertion rose, and men took their discharge when their enlistment ran out. Six hundred troops were lost to Wooster's army during the month that he commanded before the walls of Quebec.

With May's bright days, a new general came to Quebec, one with sufficient rank to take away the command from David Wooster. Major General John Thomas was General Washington's choice to meet Colonel Arnold's urgent request for a competent, effective, experienced officer to take command at Quebec. Although Thomas came victorious from the siege of Boston, and as quickly as Washington could spare him, he came too late to the Northern Army. The new general's careful study showed that, of the nineteen hundred soldiers that Wooster had on strength, only a thousand were healthy enough for duty. Further probing into the muster rolls showed Thomas that another three hundred were time-expired men, ready and eager to go home. Two hundred more of the fit men were temporarily sick as a result of inoculation for smallpox, a disease which within the month was to claim the life of General Thomas himself. On 2 May, therefore, the new general commanded five hundred effective soldiers against a city mounting one hundred and forty-eight big cannon on its strong walls, with a population of five thousand siege-tested souls, sixteen hundred of whom were under arms, and inspired by a resolute British governor general. On that day, 2 May 1776, a rumor detailed enough to be credible was abroad in the American camp: fifteen British ships had entered the mouth of the St. Lawrence, three hundred miles downstream. Given even the worst conditions of wind, tide, and weather, the fleet could be expected to disembark its regiments at Quebec City within the week. There was no time left for the American general to get control of his army, to wait for more troops to come up, to siege or storm the walls of Quebec. A sortie by the reinforced garrison of the city could soon be expected. On the morning of 5 May General John Thomas lifted the siege that, six months before, had begun with a cheer.

GOVERNOR GENERAL GUY CARLETON

Three days after Christmas, three days before Richard Montgomery died, Lieutenant Pringle of the Royal Navy called at the London office of the Secretary of State for the American Colonies, bringing with him letters from Carleton. Only thirty-six days earlier, the lieutenant had taken the oilcloth-wrapped parcel from the hand of the governor general in the beleaguered city of Quebec. Pringle's *Nancy* had made a remarkably fast eastward passage. The secretary did not keep the messenger from Canada waiting in the anteroom.

The secretary, Lord George Germaine, since 10 November 1775 had been the king's minister responsible for suppressing the armed rebellion in the thirteen united colonies—fourteen colonies, if Quebec had fallen. The naval officer, sitting erect in the visitor's chair, assured him that Carleton still held the city. The letter from the governor general asked, urged, that troops be sent in all haste. Lord

Germaine was a pompous man, and normally he was an indolent one. Now, however, he moved quickly to fill Guy Carleton's request for reinforcements.

With the support of Lord North, who led the British Parliament from the Treasury Bench, Germaine called on his cabinet colleague for regiments. They were found, some ten thousand soldiers of the infantry and the artillery, scattered in garrisons in Ireland and in England, and other troops procured by the king's agents from the greedy princelings of the tiny German states. This number of soldiers for Canada was in addition to those other troops going to help the British general cooped up in Boston.

Lord George Germaine called on the Earl of Sandwich, at the Admiralty, for transports and escort vessels to take the army safely to the St. Lawrence and upriver to Quebec, where Carleton would be waiting—if he could hold out. All through the short days of winter, the troops for Canada readied for the spring campaign. The Germans were ferried across the North Sea. The eight British regiments, recruited up, packed up, and trailing their women behind them, marched to the coastal towns where the transports waited. The fleet sailed early in the spring, to be at the mouth of the St. Lawrence when the ice went out of the river.

While the vigor and energy of England and Englishmen were massed to come to his aid, Guy Carleton waited safely within the walls of Quebec City. On the last day of the old year the Americans had tried to take the city from him, but they had failed, and in failing had squandered their resources of men. Now the rebel army was waiting for reinforcements. The siege and the defense of Quebec were at a stalemate.

For General Carleton, the new year of 1776 began four months of waiting before he could even expect the hoped-for troops from England. The first of May was the earliest date that ships from the sea could come upriver. The governor could wait. If carefully watched, there was enough food for the garrison and the civilians in the city. Fuel was short, but little forays into St. Roch (contested by the enemy) brought in enough additional supplies to carry them through. There were a few incidents and alarms, but little hazard to the town. Guy Carleton kept his city firm in its resolve to hold out through the winter.

With the coming of February the days lengthened. In March the snow blankets slipped crazily down the sloping roofs of the houses, and the slush turned to water that ran in little cascades over the steps leading down into the lower town. In April sentries on the wall watched the ice break up in the river. They saw the ice fields dwindle to cakes of ice, drifting off down the ships' channel south of Île d'Orleans.

On the first day of May, John Thomas, a new American general whose tactical movement of troops to Dorchester Heights had won the siege of Boston for the Americans, took command of the Continental troops besieging Quebec. The following morning the sentry on the Grand Battery saw, in the awakening day, the first sails of the British fleet edging up the river south of Île d'Orleans. He called the guard, who called the garrison, who raised the town. Within minutes the Grand Battery was filled with half-dressed people, wide awake in the early dawn, watching their relief come into port.

There were but three vessels in that first flotilla, Royal Navy vessels with part of the 29th Foot aboard as passengers. The transports with the English and German regiments were in the river, but were a few days behind. But the 29th, and the renewed spirits of the garrison, were enough for General Carleton to begin the reconquest of Canada. On 5 May, Guy Carleton sallied out against the Americans. That very morning, General Thomas had lifted the siege. Carleton's veterans found the rebel positions abandoned and the quarters showing all the signs of a hasty departure. Thomas and all his soldiers had fled. In the Yankee general's quarters the dinner was still warming on the back of the stove. Guy Carleton's men found it there and ate it.

THE AMERICAN PRISONERS OF WAR

The incarceration of the Americans who had been captured in the lower town began on a conciliatory note. On New Year's Day, Governor Carleton delivered a large butt of porter to the monastery where the sergeants and private soldiers of Arnold's army were kept prisoners. Each of the almost four hundred men had more than a pint of the dark, bitter brew in honor of the day that, for them, began a year without prospect. They drank, and ate the bread and cheese that also was a part of their gift from the governor, and they took hold again of hope. For the officers, thirty-odd of them, who immediately on capture had been separated from the men, Guy Carleton provided a good dinner with plenty of wine. Later, books were sent in, and the officers who were kept in a seminary, read and played cards and grew restless.

They were cheered as, one by one, their wounded were returned to them, well cared for and restored to health, though Captain Lamb's face was horribly scarred. They listened to rumors of defeats and disasters to the Continental army, tales spread deliberately by the prison guards. From the windows of their cells, they looked for help from without the walls, and toward the end of the winter their spirits rose as they heard the fire of the new American batteries open on the town. Once the American guns sent a ball that struck the walls of the prison.

For the officers, the only duty remaining to them was to escape. The first team chosen to make the attempt consisted of Captain Thayer and Captain Samuel Lockwood of Lamb's artillery. Thayer had bribed a sentry, whom he referred to as "Joe." The man was willing to help by signalling the "All Clear" from the outside. In quiet talks through the door, Joe gave the captains full information about the garrison and its plight, information that was urgently important to Colonel Arnold, besieging the city. Thayer and Lockwood first planned to let themselves out of a window and to descend by a rope of blankets the four stories to the ground. But a safer, surer way was discovered: Thayer found that by removing the planks from a barred door they could get into an attic. They would then have to jump only fourteen feet to where Joe would be waiting. With Joe giving the countersign for the night, and armed with clubs that Joe was to provide, the men expected to get to the palace gate. A jump from the wall into the deep drifts of snow thirty feet below, and they would be in St. Roch where the American army still patrolled. On 25 April, Captain Thayer was working with his penknife on the door to the attic when the British orderly officer surprised him. With polite concern, the officer led Thayer away and "to give him rest from his extraordinary labor." Simeon Thayer was shackled and imprisoned in the dark, cold 'tween decks of a schooner, moored in the St. Lawrence River. Five days later, Captains Lockwood and Hanchet, having been implicated, joined Thayer in irons on board the schooner. The officers' plot to escape had failed; Joe had been the informer.

The sergeants and privates, crowded into the upper floor of the Franciscan monastery, made their own plan of escape. Theirs was a bolder, broader plan which, once they were out of the prison, included an attack on the city from within, concerted with an attack from without. When, on 13 March, the men were moved to the Dauphin jail the chances of carrying out the revolt successfully were increased. The Dauphin stood only three hundred yards from the St. Jean gate, and as a jail it was a sieve. Sergeant Major Joseph Ashton assumed command of the prisoners and coordinated the escape and the revolt.

Through all the dreary days of winter the plan was honed by committees whispering in corners or over their cards. Divisions of men under sergeant officers were detailed to overcome the guardhouse, another division to assault the St. Jean gate, a third to turn onto the town the guns on the nearby wall. Some men were told off to set

fire to houses. This, with the infiring guns, was to be the
signal for Colonel Arnold to put in his attack. Club-like
swords were made from iron hoops, found in a disused
storeroom in the jail. The escape from the prison itself was
to be by way of a door in the partially flooded basement.
Long discussions were held as to how to free the door from
the foot of ice that had backed up against it on the inside.
That problem, too, was resolved in the mounting excitement that had to be suppressed and dissembled at each routine roll-call and inspection by the officer of the day.

The first test of the grand scheme was the escape of John
Martin, who was to carry the plans to General Arnold. At
lock-up time on the appointed day a confusion was caused,
during which Martin hid outside in the yard, where snow-
white clothes were hidden—the better to conceal him on his
furtive way over the walls of the jail and over the city
walls. When the prisoners were let into the yard next morning, there was no sign of John Martin or of the white
clothes. The conspirators rightly assumed that the messenger had escaped to Arnold.

On the night chosen by Ashton for the mass escape, an
unrelated alarm brought the guard and the field officer of
the day into the jail. An informer told the officer of the
whole plot, and the scheme of the sergeants, daring enough
to have been successful, collapsed. Punishment came the
next day. Shackles were brought in and room by room, beginning with Morgan's men, the prisoners were confined.
That night, Governor Carleton gave the arranged signal
that would alert Colonel Arnold. The Americans, chained
to their bunks in the Dauphin jail, saw the glow of the fires

through the barred windows, and heard the thumping of the guns near the St. Jean gate. The colonel did not come; Carleton's ruse had failed.

Illness, scurvy, and smallpox followed with discouragement into the prisons, where the Americans suffered the privations of the besieged city. All hope of rescue vanished when, in May, the fleet from England came with fresh regiments of British and the hireling soldiers of Germany. The jailors told the prisoners tauntingly that their comrades outside the wall had fled. The chains and handcuffs were removed from the men. Even Captains Thayer, Lockwood, and Hanchet were let out of their ship's dungeon and returned to the seminary. There was talk that a parole and an exchange of prisoners was to be effected. This was true, though it was long delayed. On 10 August, all the prisoners that remained in Quebec sailed down the St. Lawrence, bound for home.

All of Benedict Arnold's old veterans did not sail on the cartel fleet. Some eighty of them, dressed now in the Scottish regalia of Maclean's Royal Highland Emigrants, watched their comrades of the long overland march sail away to repatriation. These new recruits to the highlanders had been born in the British Isles, not in the thirteen colonies, and by a curious logic, they were more culpable than were the native Americans. They were traitors, as had been their "General," Richard Montgomery. Shortly after their capture with the rebel army Colonel Maclean had come to them in prison and had made their position perfectly clear. They had their choice: transportation "home" to England, a quick trial for treason, and hanging; or conscription into the Emigrants. For Arnold's men, trapped in the noose of legal semantics, the choice was not difficult. Alive, there was always the possibility of deserting.

Simon Fobes of Hubbard's company and Bridgewater, Massachusetts, with Reuben Johnson of Topham's and John Pollock, chose to go home by the way they had come, over the Height of Land. They escaped safely to the Great Carry. Crossing over the old road that they had helped to make, Fobes's party came again to the Kennebec. They walked beside the swift river during the fine September days, traveling slowly and easily down to the first settlement. A coasting vessel took the escape party to Boston, where the three men reported themselves to Major General Artemus Ward, commanding in the liberated city, as fit and ready for duty.

Notes on the Later Careers of Officers
in Canada in 1775

Guy Carleton, Richard Montgomery, and Benedict Arnold all achieved their measure of fame during the battle for Canada. By his gallant death, General Montgomery became well remembered. The tenacity of Governor Carleton, evidenced so clearly by his holding out in Quebec, eventually brought him a peerage. Colonel Arnold's fame was the brave fame of failure, for which he was rewarded with a brigadier general's commission. Later, bravery in success as well as failure brought other rewards to Arnold, and carried him, too, to his ultimate failure in treason and treachery.

Of the minor characters in the invasion of Canada, at least three were involved in Benedict Arnold's treason. The young gentleman from Philadelphia who scuffled in the Place des Armes in Montreal when the statue of George III was desecrated was, in all probability, David Franks. As Arnold's very elegant aide de camp, Major Franks was arrested for complicity in the plot of September 1780, but was completely exonerated by a court-martial. Lieutenant John André of the 7th Foot, captured at St. Jean, was of course the British principal in the seduction of General Arnold.

John Lamb, the distinguished artilleryman wounded and disfigured on 31 December 1775, commanded the guns at West Point in 1780, was one of the soldiers Arnold would have sold to the British.

Other officers who marched over the Height of Land and who attacked with Arnold in the snowstorm distinguished themselves in the years of war that followed. Some reached prominence in the new nation that evolved from that war.

Henry Dearborn won his lieutenant colonelcy fighting with Daniel Morgan under Arnold's command at Saratoga. From 1801 to 1809, Dearborn was Secretary of War under President Jefferson. He was commander of the army from January 1812 to June 1815, and as such, though too old to be successfully active, he fought through America's second war with England.

Aaron Burr, the nineteen-year-old volunteer of diminutive stature, during the American Revolution was a perennial follower of the successful, an energetic aide-de-camp. Burr was Vice President of the United States during Jefferson's first administration. His notoriety comes more from his implication in the strange plot to carve an empire out of the American West than from his steadfast loyalty.

Daniel Morgan continued to lead men boldly to the end of the war, from which he emerged a brigadier general. Still commanding Virginia riflemen, Morgan, with his old comrade Dearborn, turned the British flank at Saratoga, contributing largely to Arnold's second victory there. For his victory at Cowpens, North Carolina, on 17 January 1781, General Morgan received a gold medal by act of Congress.

Christopher Greene became a colonel, commanded at Red Bank on the Delaware River, and for his conduct at the Hessian attack in 1777 was given a presentation sword by the War Board. He was killed in action, 13 May 1781.

Return Jonathan Meigs also received a sword of commendation for his amphibious raid on Sag Harbor, Long Island, New York, on 1 June 1779. Meigs led one regiment, Febiger another, under General Anthony Wayne in the great night attack at Stony Point on the Hudson. He ended his life in the West as United States Commissioner to the Cherokee Indians.

Christian Febiger, the Dane who fought at Bunker Hill, at Quebec, and at Stony Point, was a colonel by rank and a brigadier by brevet when he retired from the Continental army in 1783,

Matthias Ogden, whose shoulder wound saved him from capture at Quebec, was taken prisoner as a colonel at Elizabethtown, New Jersey, in October 1780. He, too, was breveted brigadier general at the war's end.

Eleazer Oswald of Massachusetts, an early rebel patriot, first went to fight as Benedict Arnold's secretary at Fort Ticonderoga in May 1775. He was captured at Quebec, and became a friend of Lamb, in whose regiment of artillery he was commissioned lieutenant colonel in 1777. He fought with Arnold at Compo Hill, Connecticut, in April

1777; with Putnam at Fort Clinton and Fort Montgomery, New York, in October of that year, and was highly commended by Generals Knox and Lee for bravery at Monmouth, New Jersey, in June 1778. Passed over for promotion, Oswald resigned his commission and became a printer and publisher in Philadelphia. Still an ardent revolutionary, Oswald commanded an artillery regiment in the French Republican army in 1793, fighting in the battle of Jemappe. He died in New York in 1795, and is buried in St. Paul's churchyard, where in 1818 General Montgomery's bones were reinterred.

Samuel Ward became a lieutenant colonel. His granddaughter was Julia Ward Howe, who wrote "The Battle Hymn of the Republic."

David Wooster had a long career as a soldier. At the siege of Louisbourg in 1745, he was a captain in Colonel Pepperrell's regiment of British regulars, raised in Massachusetts. He served as a brigadier general of colonial troops during the French and Indian war. Sixty-four years old at the beginning of the American Revolution, he was the third ranking brigadier general in the new Continental army. He had expected to receive higher rank. Too old for an energetic, active command, and after the final failure of the Canadian campaign, he was returned to a sedentary command in his native Connecticut. Surprised by Governor Tryon's raid on Ridgefield, Wooster and Arnold turned out for the defense. Wooster was fatally wounded in the battle, 27 April 1777.

John Brown, Benedict Arnold's implacable enemy, remained always on the fringe of the army, leading state militia and irregular troops in the Northern Department. His most notable achievement was his raid on General Burgoyne's rear during the campaign of 1777. Leading Berkshire County, Massachusetts, militia, Colonel Brown was killed in action at Stone Arabia, New York, 19 October 1780.

Roger Enos, who with his three companies deserted the march to Quebec, was court-martialed and "honorably acquitted." Although vindicated, Enos resigned his Congressional commission. After serving with Connecticut militia, he removed to Vermont in 1779. He commanded Vermont troops as brigadier general in 1787, and served on the Vermont Board of War until 1792. He died at the age of seventy-nine.

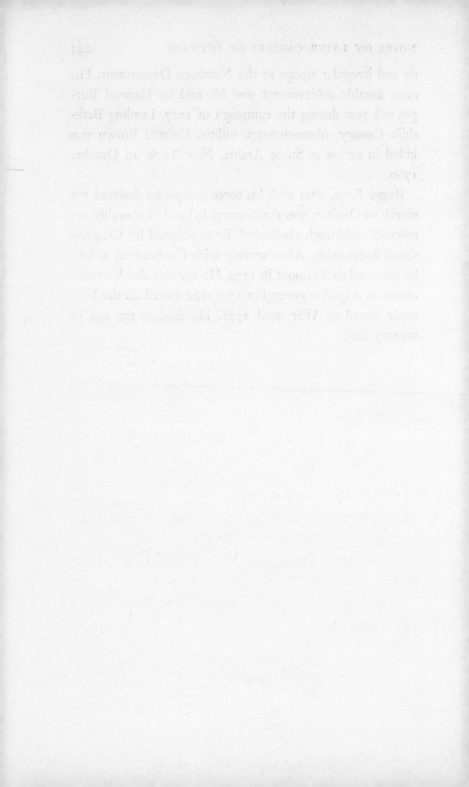

Chronology

1775

19 April	Armed rebellion begins at Lexington and Concord
10 May	Ethan Allen, with Arnold, takes Fort Ticonderoga
17 May	Arnold takes HM Sloop *Enterprise*
15 June	George Washington made commander in chief
17 June	Battle of Bunker Hill
25 June	Schuyler given command of Northern Department of the army
28 August	Montgomery leaves Fort Ticonderoga to invade Canada
5 September	Schuyler joins army which enters Canada
5-7 September	Failure of Schuyler's first attempt to lay siege to St. Jean Orders for Kennebec Expedition published by Washington

10-11 September	Failure of Schuyler's second attempt to lay siege to St. Jean
11 September	Arnold's army of the Kennebec leaves Cambridge for Newburyport
16 September	Schuyler goes sick; Montgomery takes command of army in Canada Montgomery establishes siege lines south of St. Jean
17 September	Montgomery establishes Bedel's camp north of St. Jean
19 September	Arnold's army sails from Newburyport for the Kennebec River
24 September	Ethan Allen attacks Montreal. Allen is made prisoner of war Arnold's army at Fort Weston on the Kennebec
11 October	Arnold on the Great Carry between Kennebec and Dead Rivers
18 October	Surrender of Fort Chambly on the Richelieu River
19-21 October	Tempest of rain floods the Dead River
25 October	Enos turns back
26-27 October	Wooster and reinforcements arrive at the siege of St. Jean
28 October	Arnold's army crossing the Height of Land
2 November	St. Jean surrenders to Montgomery Arnold's army crosses the Chaudière Ponds on the upper Chaudière River
5 November	Montgomery begins the march to Montreal

9 November	Arnold arrives at Point Levis, opposite Quebec
13 November	Montgomery makes victorious entry into Montreal
14 November	Arnold crosses the St. Lawrence and invests Quebec
19 November	Arnold goes to Point aux Trembles to await the arrival of Montgomery
1 December	Montgomery arrives at Point aux Trembles and takes command
5 December	Siege of Quebec begins
31 December	Attack on Quebec lower town fails; Montgomery and Arnold wounded

Notes on Sources

Twenty-seven of the soldiers who marched to Quebec over the Height of Land wrote accounts of their adventure. These have been published, in the form of journals and diaries and accounts written after the fact. Some of the latter borrow extensively from the journals for their continuity. All have their own individuality and character.

Kenneth Roberts, historian and historical novelist, published, analyzed, and annotated many of the twenty-seven accounts of Arnold's Canadian campaign in *March to Quebec*, New York, 1938.

While so many in Arnold's army wrote of their experiences, few of Montgomery's soldiers, either at St. Jean or Quebec, recorded their impressions in surviving accounts. The journals of Benjamin Trumbull and Bayze Wells, both relating to the Lake Champlain and St. Jean episodes of the Canadian campaign, are detailed and colorful.

The nine volumes of American Archives, edited by Peter Force, Washington, 1837-53, give many letters written by principals in the Congress and the army, pertinent to the campaign in 1775.

There are many secondary sources of interest and value, notably Justin H. Smith's two books, *Our Struggle for a Fourteenth Colony*, New York, 1907, and *Arnold's March from Cambridge to Quebec*, New York, 1903. John Codman's *Expedition to Quebec*, New York, 1902, rivals and is contemporary to Smith. *A Pictorial Field Book of the Revolution* by Benson J. Lossing, 2 vols., New York 1850-52, gives many details and biographical notes of interest while recounting the course of the campaign. Some of the biographies, among them James Graham's *Life of General Daniel Morgan*, New York, 1856, are of pertinent interest. Regrettably, no biographer of Benedict Arnold has come forward as yet with a plausible story of this brave soldier and despicable traitor. Biographers, and novelists such as Kenneth Roberts, have either excused or too strongly condemned, overweighing the treachery against the bravery, or the good against the bad. James Thomas Flexner has recently written of Arnold without runaway emotions. In his book "The Traitor and the Spy: Benedict Arnold and John André," New York, 1953, Flexner identifies John André as the author of "The Siege of St. Johns" (St. Jean). That narrative, in the Public Archives of Canada, is one of the very few Canadian accounts of the invasion of Canada in 1775.

The sources above, and many others relating to the time and places of the action and events, are acknowledged with gratitude for their aid in the writing of this book. Others were made available to me by the Southern Adirondack

Library System, which draws on the Central Reference Library of New York State, a library which, if necessary, will go to great lengths to find needed books. I wish to acknowledge the great assistance I have received from this Service, and, more personally, the help of Mrs. McArthur and the Staff of the Crandall Free Library in Glens Falls, New York (my home library), who made the System work for me.

I also wish to thank those others who, directly or by services, have contributed: Mrs. John Nicholas Brown, Mr. Samuel Brown, Mr. Donald Carter, the Company of Military Historians, Mr. and Mrs. Henry Foster, Mr. Clayton Gray of La Société Historique de Lac Saint-Louis, Mr. Edward Mann, Professor Frederick C. Mote, Miss Hannah Olney, Mr. David Stewart, and Mr. and Mrs. Peter G. White.

I am appreciative, too, of the patience of my wife, Harriette Jansen Bird, on our trip to the Kennebec River, the Height of Land, and the Chaudière. She bore with me in my hope for rain, sleet and snow, even a hurricane and flood, so that I might see the country over which Arnold marched in some measure as Arnold saw it. Her patience was rewarded. The sun shone, the mid-November days were mild, the country beautiful and friendly. Benedict Arnold would have liked it that way, too.

Index

James
Bay

RUPERT'S   LAND

HUDSON BAY COMPAN

LOUISIANA
(SPAIN)

M

Missouri R.

Ohio R.

New

PENNSYLVANIA

P

Mississippi R.

VIRGINIA

A. KARL